BACK

GET ᵛ IN THE KITCHEN

Bit@hes!

we're not done yet!

by jason bailin

Get BACK in the Kitchen, Bit@hes!
Copyright © 2010 by Jason R. Bailin

International Standard Book Number: 978-0-9819632-2-8
Library of Congress Control Number: 2010937448

Printed in the United States of America

Whipped & Beaten Culinary Works, Inc.
www.bitchcooks.com

To order additional copies, please contact Whipped & Beaten
Culinary Works, Inc. at www.bitchcooks.com

This book is printed on recycled-content paper that
is certified under the Sustainable Forestry Program.

WHAT'S IN IT FOR YOU, *Bit@h?*

THANKS,
Bit@h!

In addition to my family and friends that were acknowledged in my first book, this book is dedicated to you, the bitch that enjoyed the previous edition so much that you simply had to "get back in the kitchen." Your words of encouragement sent via e-mails, blog and Facebook postings, as well as during the conversations that we have engaged in, made it clear that you "hungered" for more. I thank you for being the bitches that you are, and most importantly for buying my book... again. It is because of you that I can now say that I have written a "series" of cookbooks, and there really are no words available to me to express my gratitude. From the bottom of this bitch's heart: Thank you so very, very much.

To my dear, selfless friends who journeyed with me throughout the ages to be photographed, you truly are some good bitches.

MODELS: Mona Simon, Kristin Crane, Adam Nirenberg, Justina Banks.

And, to those who helped me test the recipes that you are about to create, thank you for your trust and for being instrumental in helping to craft this work of art.

RECIPE TESTERS: Helen Bailin, Melissa and David Bailin, Mona Simon and John Cotton, Irene and Matt Sacks, Maciej Kostecki, Leslie Hudson, Angie and Shaun McKay, Kristin Crane, Rebecca and Mike Meyer, Jeff Dreher, Catherine Dillon, Holly Amatangelo, Harisha Koneru, and last, but certainly not least, Tammy and Jon H.

Thanks also to Sarita Dandamudi and the folks at Studio Snaidero Chicago, Luxe Home, Merchadise Mart for letting us use their amazing showroom to shoot the photos again, and to our extremely skilled photographer, Kari Skaflen, for again capturing the essence that is "Get in the Kitchen, BIT@HES!"

Lastly, there are two very special acknowledgements that I must make. To our newest bitch: my niece Sydney, who's smile lights up a room and who constantly provides me with new sources of inspiration; and to my grandmother, Florie, whose absence has truly been felt. She would have been proud to see you had the good sense to buy this next installment, and for that, I also dedicate this to her memory.

LEGAL
Crap!

Here is an indisputable fact: This country is filled with a bunch of money hungry bitches that will sue you for any little thing that they deem to be an inconvenience. So to that end, I want to be clear: If you screw the recipes up, hurt yourselves while attempting them, or even if you drop a bottle of wine on your foot while you are unpacking your groceries, it is not my damn fault! Don't come bitchin' to me if your spouse, partner, or friend gets mad at you for screwing the recipe up and pours hot tea on your head. You are the one that's the clumsy bitch. Got it? Whipped and Beaten Culinary Works is not responsible for your general ineptitude.

Also, if you dare try to reproduce any part of this book, I will come after you, beat you with a wooden spoon, and haunt your dreams. I can assure you that you won't be happy about that.

THIS IS WHAT YOU GET FOR SCREWING THE RECIPE UP, *Bit@h!*

ON YOUR KNEES,
Bit@h!

OK. So you've read my first masterpiece, loved the recipes and the way I treated you with the utmost respect and kindness, and decided you wanted, no, NEEDED more. Yeah, that's what I thought would happen. Admit it, there's a part of you deep down inside, that loves to be treated like the bitch you always knew you were. Plus, you loved the food you made, and the lessons you learned, and wanted to see what else I have been "cooking up." Well, we're not even close to being done. So, get your damn apron, and GET BACK IN THE KITCHEN, *Bit@h!*

Since humankind discovered fire, there have been bitches in the damn kitchen. The cavemen and women certainly roasted their fair share of woolly mammoths and probably used some dinosaur eggs to bind their first brontosaurus burgers. By the way, don't you dare write to me and tell me that cavemen weren't around when the dinosaurs were alive, because according to the damn Flinstones, dinosaurs played a huge part in pre-historic cuisine... so suck it, bitch.

Throughout the ages, humans have perfected their culinary skills, moving food preparation indoors from the caves, to the roman coliseums, right into the kitchens of the colonies. The modern kitchen is chock-full of appliances and gadgets that help the contemporary cook create amazing dishes (llke the one's you are about to learn). We now have amazing contraptions like our convection ovens, exotic utensils and modern marvels like those damn hand blenders that you see on infomercials at 3 a.m. (Don't get me started on those stupid bitches! I would love to put them in their cheap oven gizmos and "Set it and Forget it!")

Anyway, I digress. Since the culinary arts have been around for thousands and thousands of years, I have decided to dedicate this next book of the series, to all the bitches who worked tirelessly in the kitchens of yesteryear. After all, if not for them, I wouldn't be as awesome a cook as I am today.

OK... now back to the book. You'll be happy to know that I have been reviewing your feedback. While most of it was utterly useless crap, there were a few pearls of wisdom I thought I should incorporate into this next installment. I have added more recipes. That means more entrées, appetizers, sides, and this time... I even included a couple of desserts. Lucky freaking you.

Rest assured, the same rules apply so your feeble mind won't get confused. Each recipe is again rated with the following system:

DUMB *Ass*

These are meant for the culinary challenged. Even you can make these meals, dumb ass.

THE LITTLE CHEF THAT *Could*

I think you can, I think you can.

ARE YOU F%@KING KIDDING *Me?*

These might take a little extra time—and a brain. While these recipes are definitely a challenge, they can be mastered by all. Don't be a wimpy piece of trash. Try one.

Also, each recipe is still accompanied by the "Words of Wisdom" section where I provide you with some tips on why the meal tasted good as well as the "S&M" (Sides & More) section where I provide guidance on pairing appetizers, salads, and sides with the entrée you have selected.

This time around however, I plan to take it up a level. Really test your skills and see if your miniscule brain matter retained any knowledge from the first book. The recipes are going to be slightly more complex, slightly more creative, and slightly more awe inspiring. I'm not sure some of you will be able to handle them, but those that triumph will

8

earn my respect. Well, on second thought, let's not go that far. I don't think I will ever respect any of your bitch-asses. After all, you bought a cookbook called "Get in the Kitchen, BIT@HES!"... twice.

In addition to using the American staples such as beef, pork and chicken, this time around we are going to use some uncommon foods that you probably wouldn't normally pair together, or even cook with. This may be out of your comfort zone of meat and potatoes, but I've got one thing to say. Deal with it, bitch. Try something new damn it! Also, I don't remember asking for your opinion.

One big addition to this book is a chapter dedicated to cooking lessons. In this section, I am going to teach your sorry little ass some basic cooking techniques and jargon so you don't look and sound like an idiot anymore.

I have also expanded on two chapters from the last book: "So, You're Still Too Damn Lazy to Start from Scratch?" and "Learning to Love Your Leftovers." I have been working indefatigably for you bitches and have developed a handful of more tips on how to use your leftovers and packaged foods to make amazing meals. I thought you should know about them. Pretty nice of me huh? Yeah, whatever. Like I care what you think.

As a result of all of this, I believe I have created what has to be the most important culinary work of our time, and I have to say you are one lucky bitch. You certainly got a steal here, and you're welcome.

OK bitch. Enough of this banter. Are you ready to learn a few techniques? Yeah, I thought so. Turn the damn page, let's get started.

• • • • • • • • •

IT'S TIME TO BOOGIE DOWN, *Bit@h!*

YOU ARE SUCH A TOOL,
Bit@h!

In the last book, I talked to you about the basic food ingredients and spices that you needed to have in your house at all times. However, I neglected to tell you the utensils that you should own in order to cook. Big mistake. I had some of you stupid bitches writing in to me asking all kinds of questions about what to use to cook your meals. Questions like "If I don't have a ladle, can I use my hands to scoop out hot soup?" filled my e-mail box… I mean, come on bitches. Go out and get the proper tools damn it! Here are the basics of what you should stock your kitchen with.

Spatula: If you don't have one of these, well, then you don't deserve to even own a copy of this book. You don't deserve to breathe same air as the rest of us. Go to the store and buy one.

Tongs: If you really want to start cooking, you're gonna need a pair of tongs. Tongs are great for moving around cuts of meat in a frying pan, folding pasta in with sauce, and they also come in quite handy in the bedroom.

Casserole Dish: A kitchen without a casserole dish is just plain wrong, bitch. You absolutely need one to make any sort of home cooked meals whether it be for the holidays, or a casual family dinner. Casseroles are awesome 'cause you just throw a ton of crap in and bake. If you are taking care of an elderly relative, they can also be utilized as a bed pan, should you need one. If you don't have a proper casserole dish, get one. It's that damn simple.

Semi-Deep Frying Pan with a Cover: You need one larger, deeper frying pan. This is useful for braising and making sauces. It also does a hellu-va lot more damage than a smaller specimen to a burglar or a spouse should they get out of line and deserve a smack upside the head.

Whisk: I used to use a fork to beat an egg or mix things. Then I spent the 5 bucks on a whisk. Let me tell you bitch... worth every damn penny. Eggs are beaten in half the time and because of its design, everything is blended evenly. And if you thought the tongs made a great sexual device, you have no freaking idea about what a whisk can do.

Chopping Knife: I don't use any other knife in my kitchen as much as my chopping blade. It is my best friend. And last year when I was at the bris of my good friend's son and the Mohel didn't show up... it was very helpful.

Good Set of Cutting Knives: It is so much easier to cut things with knives that don't fall apart. When I was younger and naive, I got sucked into one of those infomercials and bought a set of "chef knives." I was stupid. Very, very stupid. The day after I used them for the first time, I promptly donated them to my local charity resale shop so some other schmoe could make the same mistake. I then went out and spent the money on a proper set. If you cook a lot, get some proper knives. This is my best advice.

Colander: When I got out of college, I bought this little strainer in place of a colander because it, and I, was cheap. It took me three second-degree burns and a floor full of food to replace it with a proper colander. Not only is it easy for draining pasta and vegetables, but sifting for gold in the backyard is a breeze as well. Go out and get one if you don't have one damn it!

Ladle: No, you can't just use your hands to scoop out hot soup. Nuff said.

Good Cutting Board: As I said, I used to be a cheap bitch and bought one of those small-ass cutting boards because it was five bucks as opposed to fifteen for the really big and sink-attachable one. If you cook even half as much as I do, spend the damn money. It makes life a helluva lot easier and your countertops a helluva lot cleaner.

Stock Pot, Sauce Pots and a Good Frying Pan: If you're gonna cook, you need some good pots and pans. A stock pot will help you create broths, soups, and help you braise large pieces of meat. Sauce pots are great for… well, making sauces. And after I am done with you, you will be making a lot of those. So, stop using the small, insufficient pots and pans you have around the house and get something that will work.

Food Processor: During my first few years as a post-college bachelor, I tried to use my blender as a food processor. You know, the one I used to make my Margaritas in. Yeah. Didn't work. At all. For proper food prep, you need a proper processor. Now, there are a bunch on the market that are affordable. The more expensive ones are awesome, but the cheaper ones will definitely do.

UNNECESSARY, BUT WORTH IT, *Bit@h*

Crockpot: I love my crockpot more than sex. There is nothing like coming home from work to a house smelling of chili or braised meats. Plus, it's so damn easy to make an amazing meal with one of these contraptions. The inventor should have gotten the Nobel Prize for "Being So Damn Awesome."

So bottom line is this. If you don't own a crockpot, get off your damn ass and get one. That's all I have to say about that.

Tenderizer: About a decade ago, I wanted to make some chicken parmigiana. Up until this time, I had simply butterfly-cut the breasts to make them thin, dredged them in flour and pan-fried them. However, this time was different. I had just experienced the most delectable chicken cutlet at a restaurant a few weeks prior. It was so thin, that I almost mistook it for veal and wanted to recreate it. The problem was that I didn't have a meat tenderizer to pound it with. So I thought I would improvise and got out my toolbox. I wrapped the chicken in plastic wrap and proceeded to take my hammer to the breast. Well, after making three, quarter-sized holes right through the meat rendering it unusable, I decided to go out and get a tenderizer. If you're planning to step up your game in the kitchen, and make restaurant quality cutlets at home, I would recommend you get one too.

Dutch Oven: Listen, bitch. I am not talking about when you are in bed, and release gas under the covers and proceed to seal your partner's head in there. (Although, if you haven't tried that yet...I recommend it. The bitches really go wild for that sort of sh*t.) What I am talking about though, is the large, deep, coverable oven-safe dishes. While I do a lot of my braising on the stove in a deep pan, I find it is not ideal for a large roast or considerable quantities of meat. When I am making dinner for the bitches I call friends, I need to make a little more. If you have a family, you should invest in a Dutch Oven. It's so versatile and can go from the stove for browning, to the oven for braising. I would recommend you get one bitch!

Oven-Safe Cast Iron Skillet: OK, I'll admit you can live without this, but in the next chapter I am going to teach you about pan-roasting and you won't be able to do it without one. I wouldn't want you to feel left out, bitch.

Lemon Juicer: There is nothing in this world more disheartening and foul than biting down into some of my most delectable dishes only to encounter a stray lemon seed. After years of tasting the hard and excruciatingly bitter flavor, I finally decided to go out and pick up one of those amazingly handy lemon juicers. You know, the ones you place half the lemon in, close it tightly and start to squeeze in order to liberate its sweet and sour nectar. I have not had to endure another seed since.

Pizza Cutter: I have to say that being a cheap bitch, the pizza cutter was not on my list of items to purchase when I first started cooking for myself. However, one drunken night I walked down to the grocery store to purchase a frozen pizza. As I was walking out, I passed through the utensil aisle, and with the frozen mound of crust, sauce and cheese in one hand and a six pack in the other (I didn't want to lose my buzz after all), my eyes fixated on a pizza cutter. By the way, if you've never been GSUI at 2 a.m.(Grocery Shopping Under the Influence), get a group of friends together, have a few shots and do it. It's a damn good experience. Anyway, my eyes fixated on the pizza cutter, I picked it up, and have loved the purchase ever since. I use it to cut my pizzas, dough when I make dumplings, won tons, fresh pasta, you name it. While it certainly isn't a necessity, it's been a loving and valued addition to my kitchen.

Deep Frying Slotted Spoon: I don't deep fry a lot, but some days when I am feeling low because one of you bitches have annoyed me, I just want to make some deep fried, artery clogging, fat building goodness. However, without a proper deep frying slotted spoon to scoop the "Food of the Gods" out of the hot oil, I was always left with a burn or a mess on the counter. I would get one.

There are definitely some great utensils out there that I haven't mentioned. You can spend a whole damn week shopping for stuff. However, I think you can live with these to start. If you have another that you feel should be on the list... well, I don't really give a sh*t, write your own damn book. Moving on.

CULINARY SCIENCES:
ONE-OH-*Bit@h!*

OK... since you are all such crappy little low-life bitches, I thought you could use some pointers. I mean, really start learning what to do in the kitchen. The oven isn't just a place to store your dish towels, or your pots and pans, or even your sex toys. It actually serves a real and practical purpose, and performs this awe-inspiring act: It takes raw ingredients and, get this... heats them up, blending their flavors to create not just edible, but sensational meals. But first you have to turn the damn thing on, bitch. Same goes for your stove-top, and even your freakin' crockpot. In this section, I am going to attempt to educate your meager brains by teaching you some cooking techniques that will not only help you to make the recipes in this book, but also allow you to create amazing meals on your own.

Now, I consider myself a great educator. When I was about 13, my brother and I would study for tests together. I had a very effective technique. If my brother got a question wrong, I simply slammed a hard textbook onto his hand. Harsh, but successful, damn it! Now unfortunately, I can't be there in person to brand your hands with a hot spoon if you screw something up, but if you have someone you love and trust, maybe they can stand in.

HOW TO DEGLAZE A *Pan*

I thought I would start here because it is simple (so you can probably handle it), and it's a procedure used in a lot of the other techniques I will be talking about. Deglazing is just a fancy term for getting all the leftover food bits "unstuck." You see, those food bits that are stuck to a pan after sautéing or pan-frying are full of luscious flavor! Many chefs use the deglazing technique to help create awesome sauces for their main dish.

As I said, it is very simple. After you're done sautéing or pan-frying your dish, you will notice the extra food particles stuck to the pan. I like to call these "super tasty bits." Cute and cuddly huh? Well, I do get a little soft at times. Deal with it, bitch.

I digress. When you deglaze, you are aiming to loosen these "super tasty bits" in order to use them in a sauce or gravy. All you have to do is add some form of liquid. I like to use a little wine. I find it adds a great flavor to any sauce I am going to make. However, you can also use stock, broth or even a bit of water to liberate the particles as well. All you have to do is add enough liquid to coat the bottom of the pan or pot and start stirring. One thing, though. And this is very important, especially for a feeble bitch like you. If you use any type of alcohol, be sure to take the pan off the heat first, dumb ass. 'Cause if you don't you're gonna remove your damn eyebrows when the alcohol catches fire.

SAUTEING THE *Sausage*

Listen up bitches, because this is the most important technique that I can teach your sorry ass. When you learn how to sauté properly, this easy technique will allow you to make meals out of basically anything you have lying around your kitchen. You can also use this technique to keep the kids in line. A couple of sautéed fingers never killed anyone.

SO, WHAT THE F%@K IS *Saute?*

First, a little linguistics lesson. The word sauté is from the french word "sauter" meaning "to jump." The reason why it has been adapted to describe this method of cooking is because the object is to keep the food moving in the heat of the pan. If you don't keep the food moving, then you will f%@k it up, and fail like the stupid little bitch that you are. When you sauté, you use a fatty substance like butter or oil to transfer the heat of the pan to the food ingredients. There are four important tips I can give you so that you can be successful:

STEPS FOR *Sautéing*

1) Make sure the pan is heated before applying the oil and the food ingredients. This is important for three reasons. One, you want to make sure the fat doesn't break down as it heats up. Two, you want to make sure the pan is uniformly hot. And three, if you are cooking meat of some sort, it will sear in the juice and allow the end product to be a lot more succulent.

2) Keep the food moving with either a wooden spoon or other utensil that won't scratch the pan. Professional chefs might toss the food around the pan. But you, my dear, are not a professional chef. So don't you dare try to do this. You will end up with a floor full of oily food or worse, in the hospital with third-degree burns on your face. Don't be a stupid bitch. Use the damn spoon.

3) Use only enough oil or butter to coat the bottom of the pan. This is not deep-frying, bitch! Don't drown the damn food. Just give it enough fat so that you can transfer the heat of the pan.

4) Pay attention to the ingredients damn it! If you are using a mix of vegetables and meats, know that they cook at different speeds. I like to always start with what I call a "flavoring" vegetable like onion, garlic or shallots, then follow with the meat, and eventually the rest of the vegetables. This way the oil will be flavored before I put the meat in, and the rest of the vegetables won't be overcooked. Obviously this may vary if you are following a recipe. Also, make sure the vegetables are similar in size. This will help you to cook them uniformly.

Don't confuse sautéing with pan-frying where you use more oil, keep the food whole (don't chop it), and let the food sit. We will talk more about pan-frying next, so hold your damn horses.

BUTTER OR *Oil?*

I can just hear your whining little voices... "Should I use butter or oil? And if it is oil, what kind of oil?...Oh, and why use different types of oil?…wah wah wah!" Just stifle yourself for a moment and let me talk. When I am cooking different cuisines, I use different types of fat. The difference is the flavor and the "smoking point." No, I'm not talking about the point where you light up bitches. In this case, it's the instance where the oil begins to smoke and therefore burn. Butter has a lower smoking point than oil, but a richer flavor. Therefore, when you use butter, keep it on a lower heat. Olive Oil has a lower smoking point than vegetable oil, but also a heartier flavor. So, to keep it simple, here is a little guideline I use… and hence, you should too.

OIL OR BUTTER, *Bit@h?*
Rich Cuisines like French—Butter
Italian and Mediterranean Cuisine—Olive Oil
Asian Cuisine—Sesame Oil
Mexican Cuisine—Vegetable, Canola Oil

If in doubt, I will fall back on the olive oil. A lot of the flavor of the oil you use will fade as it cooks, so I just tend to go with the healthier of the bunch, and that is Olive Oil. However, I do find that no matter how long I cook the food, Sesame Oil is the best in Asian dishes. Once you get the hang of it, you can also combine butter and oil to come up with a great rich flavor as well. Try it out, bitch. The worst that can happen is you burn the house down.

SO HOW DAMN HOT SHOULD THE PAN *Be?*

Listen to you... all full of stupid questions. Well simply put, I like to set the pan to a medium heat before I apply the fat of choice. This will ensure that the fat won't burn as soon as you put it in the pan, and provides a good starting point to increase the heat if necessary (which is usually necessary).

TIPS FOR *Sautéing*

When I sauté, I preheat the pan on medium, add the oil or butter and let that heat up for about 30-60 seconds. I then add the onions and garlic. At this point, I raise the heat to medium-high and flavor with a dash of salt and pepper. The salt helps the onion and garlic flavor to "sweat" into the oil. After about a minute or two, I add the meat, and if there is some liquid flavor (like soy sauce, wine, or vinegar) I will add that after the meat has been sautéing for 45 seconds or so. It is important to add any liquid flavor after you have put some ingredients in the pan. This is so that the pan can cool down a bit and the liquid won't splatter and kill someone. At this point I will start to add any other vegetables I plan to use. I find that this gives the meat the best flavoring and allows the vegetables to cook properly.

So that's it, bitch. That is how to sauté your man's meat…er… I mean sauté some meat. Don't f%@k it up.

PAN-*Frying*

As promised bitch, here's everything you need to know about pan-frying. Pan-frying is a method of cooking where you place large cuts of meat, fish, chicken or vegetables into a shallow pan and let them sit in the fat medium, rather than move it around like you would do when sautéing. Here are the differences. Learn 'em bitch!:

DIFFERENCE BETWEEN SAUTÉ AND PAN-*Frying*

1) When you sauté, you cut the food into smaller pieces, rather than leave it whole (i.e. a chicken breast or pork chop) when you pan-fry.

2) You will leave the food to sit in the fat and merely flip it once to cook both sides, as opposed to moving it around the pan when sautéing.

3) You will most likely use a little more oil so the food doesn't burn.

WHY THE HELL SHOULD I PAN-*Fry*?

Well, bitch, there are a few benefits of pan-frying. Firstly, it tastes pretty damn good. Secondly, you use a helluva lot less oil or fat than if you were to use another frying method such as deep-frying. This is a good thing because you will not clog your arteries as fast. It also results in a lot less calories than deep-frying so you won't get as fat and subsequently... get dead.

SO, HOW DO I DO *It?*

Well, it's pretty damn simple. If you screw this up… well then, you're more of an idiot than I previously thought. That being said, the most common fails with this method are A) not using enough oil and B) using too high a temperature setting. That will result in you burning your food. Don't be a dumbass and burn your food. Here are the steps:

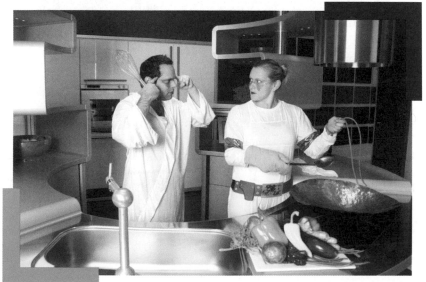

STEPS FOR PAN-*Frying*

1) Prepare your meat or vegetable by seasoning it, and if you're not a lazy bitch, lightly flouring it. The flour will help to form a crust on the meat and sear in the juices, so it's worth the extra two seconds of prep.

2) Heat the pan.

3) Add the oil or fat medium. You should use enough oil to completely cover the bottom of the frying pan and let it rise about a quarter of an inch high.

4) Let the oil heat completely by setting it to medium high.

5) Place your food in the pan and don't move it around. Monitor the heat so you don't burn the food.

6) Flip the food to ensure it is cooked on both sides and cooked through.

Usually, you will accompany the food with some sort of sauce to enhance the flavor. Later in this chapter, I teach you how to deglaze the pan and use the "super tasty bits" to make great sauces. However, you'll have to wait patiently until I get to that section. Well, I guess you can also be an unruly bitch and skip to it. Although, in order to avoid bodily harm, I would recommend you just wait.

PAN-*Roasting*

OK bitch. Do you want to act like a professional chef and impress the dildos you call friends? Well here is a great technique that combines pan-frying and roasting. Hence, it's called pan-roasting. This is one technique that saves time and produces a great finish for thick cuts of meat.

It involves searing the meat first and then placing the meat still in the pan, directly into the oven to finish. You will most likely accompany the finished product with a delightful sauce of your choosing. You like that, huh? "Delightful Sauce." That was my sarcasm coming out. Anyway. Back to your sorry ass and pan-roasting.

As a result of searing the meat and then using the convection heat of the oven, pan-roasting enables your pathetic ass to speed up the cooking process. Depending on the size, thickness and hardness of your meat, you can get dinner on the table within a half hour at most. So it's a great technique for those times that you want to create a special meal for your significant other with the hope of getting into her pants, as well as when you just come home from work and don't have much time, but desire something thick and juicy to insert into your mouth. Very versatile, huh?

SO WHAT THE F%@K DO I NEED FOR THIS "PAN-ROASTING" *Crap?*

Well, first and foremost, you need an oven ready pan. Cast iron works the best. Make sure any handles are oven safe. Don't try using a pan with handles made of plastic or plastic coating because it can be time consuming when you have to clean the melted disaster off the bottom of the oven rack. Don't be a stupid bitch. Use your damn common sense.

Secondly, you will need an oven. I find that an oven works better than placing the food on your back patio and allowing the sun to bake it. You will too. Oven mitts would be a good thing to have at this point as well, because when you reach for the pan that has been sitting in 350 degrees without them, you might feel a slight warm and tingly sensation.

SO HOW DO I DO THIS HERE "PAN-*Roasting?*"

Damn, you really are a redneck piece of trash, huh? "This here pan-roasting?" Who the hell talks like that?? At any rate, it is really very simple. Here are the steps:

STEPS FOR *Pan-Roasting*

1) First pre-heat your oven to 350 degrees. Do this first because you want to make sure it is at that temperature when the meat is ready to be inserted.

2) Prepare your cast iron pan by preheating that on the stove-top as well.

3) When the pan is hot, add an oil with a high smoking point. You can use vegetable oil.

4) When the oil is heated, and damn it, not one second before it is thoroughly heated, bitch... add your thick, juicy, and seasoned slab of meat. Make sure you season it before you sear it. You can also lightly flour it as well.

5) Sear it on all sides for approximately two minutes each. It should be nice and golden brown at this point.

6) Place the entire pan in the oven for anywhere between five and twenty minutes, depending on the type, cut, and thickness of the meat. Use a meat thermometer to tell when it reaches the recommended temperature for that particular meat.

7) Finally, you can deglaze the pan used in order to make a great sauce.

BRAISING THE *Bit@h*:

WHY THE HELL SHOULD I *Braise?*

Braising can be great for tough cuts of meat like lamb shanks, pot roasts, brisket and even chicken. Although, you really can braise anything you like. I like to braise a variety of foods from meats to fruits and vegetables. Some people will just stick to the tough cuts of meat, but I say f%@k 'em. If it tastes and feels good, do it.

When you braise, you are basically searing and browning the food and then simmering it in a flavorful liquid for what can be a very long time. But oooohhhh so worth the wait. Ever have braised ribs? Braised meat that just falls apart right when your fork touches it? Damn, my mouth is watering just writing about this. I may have to go take a private moment.

OK, I am back and have regained my composure. A quick meat rubbing will do that. No... I literally just applied a spice rub to a roast that I am about to braise. Get your damn mind out of the gutter bitch.

OK, back to braising. Braising is a great technique for a few reasons:

BENEFITS OF *Braising*

1) You only have to use one pan or Dutch Oven.

2) You can use cheaper cuts of meat and they turn out amazing.

3) You leave the meal to be for hours and hours. You don't have to tend to it and can get some other things done like cleaning your mess of a house, watching your stories on TV, or even going a few rounds with your lover.

4) With the leftover juices you have a great broth base for soup (just freeze it and use it at a later date) or gravy which you can put directly on the meat.

MOMMA NEEDS SOME FOOD, *Bit@h!*

So now that we've gone over the reasons of why to braise your thick, juicy meat, we can get into the mechanics. Here are four quick steps to help you.

MECHANICS OF *Braising*

1) Brown it! I like to either marinate the meat overnight or spice it (can use any spices but salt and pepper are basic) right before I brown it. Be sure to sear each side of the meat until it begins to form a golden brown crust (hence "browning"). I use the pot, pan, or dutch oven that I will be utilizing to braise the meat. That way all the "super tasty bits" that get stuck to the bottom are incorporated into the braising liquid.

2) Once the meat is browned, I set it aside. I then deglaze the pan by pouring a bit of the wine, marinade, or broth that I will use to braise, into the cooking device.

3) Place the meat back in the pot and pour the cooking liquid until it reaches a little more than halfway up the food. Cover and simmer either in an oven or on the stove for 2-8 hours (depending on the food). For vegetables and fruits, the time is a lot shorter than for meats.

4) Use the excess liquid to serve as an au jus or make into gravy or a sauce by adding butter and flour and stirring.

You can braise anything, really. The meats mentioned above (ribs, roasts, shanks) are all great for braising. I also like to braise them with vegetables like potatoes, onions, carrots, etc. Root vegetables like potatoes, carrots and beets work great for braising because they start out tough, and can stand a good soak to get them soft…just like you bitch. Apples, pears and other hard fruits are great to braise with meat because they give a great flavor to the end product and also taste great on the side afterwards. I would normally use peaches, apples, pears or maybe even pineapple to braise with. Just make sure you add the vegetables and the fruits in the last hour before you finish because they require a lot less time than the meat. If you add onions and potatoes at the beginning they will most likely disintegrate right into the liquid by the end.

Another tip is to freeze the leftover juices from braising. You can use them again in sauces, gravies, soups, and stews. So, that's it. That is braising. Have fun with it… and again, don't f%@k it up bitch!

● ● ● ● ● ● ● ●

SPEAKING OF STEW *Bit@h!*

So you've got some vegetables and meat that're gonna go bad if you don't use them soon. What the hell do you do with them? You stew 'em bitch! A great stew can be a hearty meal or a great mid-winter comfort. And it's pretty damn easy to make. You can also freeze it and then heat it up on those nights that you're an even lazier bitch than normal.

Stews are very similar to braises. You throw the damn food into a pot, fill it with some sort of savory liquid and simmer it for a long time. The main differences are these:

- In a stew, you use cut-up vegetables and meat; in a braise, you typically use the whole cut of meat.

- In a stew, you immerse the food in the broth; in a braise, you submerge the food halfway.

WHAT THE HELL SHOULD I *Stew?*

As with braising, you get the best bang for your buck when you use the toughest and cheapest cuts of meat. Shanks, briskets, chuck, and chicken are all great candidates. As far as vegetables go: root vegetables and other hard vegetables such as celery are perfect for stewing.

First of all, remember who you're talking to. I am the bitchmaster, and you my friend, are the bitch!

PREPARING A *Stew*

1) Dredge chunks of meat in flour (this will also help to thicken the stew later on.)

2) Saute some onion and/ or garlic in a pot.

3) In the same pot, sear meat on all sides. When sufficiently browned, add the vegetables and sauté for a couple of minutes.

4) Deglaze the pot with whatever liquid you plan to use. You can leave the meat in for this step or take it out. I find it's easier with the meat in.

5) Pour in enough liquid to just cover the meat, and bring it to a simmer. You can either stew it on the stove-top on a very low setting, or in a Dutch Oven or cast-iron, coverable pot in the oven. But again, as with pan roasting, don't be a stupid bitch and use a pot that is not oven-safe.

6) Cover tightly, and let simmer for the duration of the recipe.

7) If the liquid is still not thick enough, you can use a slurry (cornstarch in water and mixed thoroughly—about a teaspoon of cornstarch in a half a cup of water). You can also use a roux (equal parts butter and flour) to thicken the liquid as well.

Listen, I am not gonna tell you again. You are the bitch here! After stewing for a long time, some of the vegetables in the stew are gonna basically disintegrate. You can do one of the following:

1) Throw the damn things out and replace them in the last 40 minutes with fresh ones. However, this will make you a wasteful bitch, so I recommend this next option:

2) Remove them, toss 'em in your freakin' food processor and purée them. Then replace them back into the stew. This will help thicken the stew and retain the flavor.

USING A CROCKPOT TO STEW AND *Braise*

As I mentioned in the previous chapter, I love my crockpot more than sex. It is one of the most useful appliances in my kitchen and I love to just throw some crap in there, turn it on, and come back hours later to an amazing meal.

Here's the thing, though. An important step in stewing and braising is browning the food before you simmer it. When you use a crockpot, you can't really brown the food inside of it. So, what you can do is brown the food in a pan on the stove, place it in the crockpot, deglaze the pan and then pour it, and the cooking liquid into the crockpot.

BRINE IT *Bitch!* or
MARINATE YOUR *Meat!*

Chefs tend to brine and marinate meat to make the end result more tender, moist, and flavorful. I have to admit that I tend to marinate a lot more than brine, but both are very useful in tenderizing and flavoring your meat before you cook it. And let me tell you bitch, these techniques work. They work wonders!

First, let's give you a few mechanics so your small minds understand exactly what is happening when you brine and marinate. When you brine, you are adding flavor and moistness through osmosis. Basically, the salt mixture is mixing with the meat to break down the fibers and help retain moisture. When you marinate, you are using acid to tenderize the meat. That is the basic difference. That's all the science I think you can handle, so we will leave it at that.

Brining is very simple. All you have to do is make a salt water solution and soak the meat. Marinating is slightly more complicated in the fact that you have to prepare a great flavored acidic-based sauce first, so it takes slightly more brain cells. If you don't think you can handle following a marinade recipe, then brine it, bitch!

I find that marinating overnight works best, but if you don't have that much time, 2-4 hours can work as well. If you are brining though, you should take notice of the times. A simple rule of thumb that I find works best is to brine the meat for one to two hours per pound. However, in the case of whole birds like turkeys and chicken, overnight is optimal.

HOW TO BRINE A *Bit@h*

When brining, you are making a simple salt water solution. Although, I find that adding some brown or white sugar to the mix helps to temper the salt. I have even used some honey or maple syrup and they really help to soften up the brine as well. To make a brine, simply bring water to a boil and add salt and sugar. Then, when the salt and sugar has dissolved, let it cool. If you don't let it cool before you immerse your sweaty meat into it, you will begin the cooking process and your dish will turn out salty. The brine and the meat should be at the same temperature when you submerge it.

BRINE IT *Bit@h!*

1) Cool the brine! It should be at the same temperature as the meat.

2) Fully submerge the meat.

3) Brine it for a good amount of time or its f%@king useless.

4) Finally. Know your salt! Salts are not created equal damn it! A cup of Kosher Salt has less sodium than table salt. This is because there are a lot more granules in table salt as it is not "clumped" together. I find that Kosher salt works best in brines. If you use table salt, lower the amount you use.

SO, HOW MUCH DAMN SALT SHOULD I *Use?*

Well, bitch. So glad you asked, because I love giving these types of answers to a sub-par human just to see them get confused. The answer is: It depends! Ha! A basic rule I follow is to use between ½ and ¾ of a cup of kosher salt for every gallon of water. This will depend if you add any other herbs and spices, but that ratio should always work well. If you use table salt, I would use about ⅓ to ½ a cup.

HOW TO MARINATE YOUR SWEATY *Meat*

OK, on to marinating. In case your insufficient mind didn't retain the information above, marinating uses some sort of acidic solution to tenderize and flavor the meat. So in this case, you are looking to create a sauce that adds flavor and breaks down the fibers using wine, vinegar, citrus juice, or some other form of flavorful acid. Then, I like to submerge the meat into the marinade for anywhere between 5 and 24 hours. I find the longer the meat is submerged, the better.

If you ever just need a simple marinade, I find a combination of soy sauce and balsamic vinegar, some spices, and a little hot sauce work well with all meats.

So that is all I can say about brining and marinades. Good luck with that.

SAUCY BABY, *Saucy*

So, we have been talking a helluva lot about deglazing pans to make sauces, but unless you really know a thing or two about creating sauces, you're sh*t out of luck. So, relax, stop palpitating, and listen. I am going to give you a few pointers so that you can make and create sauces that your friends, lovers, and family will want to be bent over and bitch-slapped for.

There really are four basic ingredients to making sauces that sing. 1) Butter or oil to sauté, 2) wine to deglaze, 3) stock or broth, and 4) a butter/flour mixture called a roux. Using this base you can add other ingredients such as spices, vegetables, cream, and even bits of meat to make sauces that are so outstanding, you will orgasm right there in front of the stove while tasting them. Just make sure not to get any orgasm juice in the finished product, I find that it can make the sauce a tad bit bitter.

BASIC STEPS TO PREPARING A *Sauce*

1) Sauté a pungent vegetable or herb such as onion, garlic, shallot, leeks, etc. in oil (I prefer olive oil for sauces) or butter.

2) Once the onions, etc. start to brown and stick to the pan, deglaze the pan with some wine. If you are making a light sauce, use white wine, if you are making a darker sauce you can use a red, Marsala, or even a Sherry wine.

3) As the wine reduces (loses both volume and alcohol), add any vegetables or meat bits that you were planning to add. This can be mushrooms, carrots, broccoli, etc. If you are feeling creative and energetic, I find that puréeing the vegetables gives the sauce the flavor without a "chunky" sensation.

4) Add the stock or broth. If you are making a sauce for red meat, use a red meat stock or broth like beef or lamb, if you are making it for chicken, use a chicken stock or broth. You can also use a vegetable broth for both.

5) Add the spices, cover, and simmer for a few minutes.

6) When all of the flavors have been melded, add the roux. For a simple roux, I dip pats of butter in flour and coat all sides. The rule of thumb is to add equal parts butter, to equal parts flour.

7) Stir, cover, and let simmer until it thickens.

And there you have a basic sauce.

Now, you ask "Well, what the hell? You talked about deglazing the pan after sautéing and pan-roasting in the other sections. How do I use that, dumb ass?" First of all, don't you dare call me dumb ass, bitch! Secondly. Pipe the hell down. I was just giving you the basics. We will now talk about how to make a sauce after making your main dishes.

It's really very simple. After you are done with your sauté or pan-roasting, you simply deglaze the pan with some wine or broth. At this point, you can start at step three.

Also, when you are done braising or roasting, you can use the left-over liquids to make sauces and gravies as well. Simply add some flour and stir until the lumps have been removed. If you are making gravy, add more flour to make it thicker, less if you're making a simple sauce.

That's it. That simple. Good luck bitch.

ROAST THIS, *Bit@h!*

Roasting is so damn easy, that I considered not even putting a section about the proper ways to roast in the book. Then I remembered who I was dealing with, so thought it couldn't hurt.

The biggest risk in roasting is the meat or food drying out. We've all had Auntie Mae's or even Uncle Tom's Thanksgiving turkey where it felt like we were eating cotton balls and gravy. Well, this was probably because he roasted it at either too low or too high a temperature. That stupid bitch. Too low and the meat doesn't seal and keep the juices in. Too high and, well, it just goes dry.

The basic steps to roasting are as follows: Start with a high heat to seal the meat and keep the juices inside. Then after 10-20 minutes, lower the heat to finish it. Basting will be helpful to keep the meat juicy if you are making a pork or beef roast, but really just serves to make the skin of a whole bird look nice and golden brown. Either way, keep basting to a minimum to keep the heat in the oven, and only do it in the last hour of cooking.

When roasting whole birds, I find that if you start with the breast down and then turn it over for the last half hour, the juices will re-distribute in the breast making it one juicy mother f%@ker.

Also, be sure to keep all the juices at the end for a gravy. You can use half for gravy and then freeze the rest for a sauce, or to make a soup, or stew out of later on.

So there you have it, bitches. Just a few basic cooking methods to help you in your culinary journey. With these as a base, you can pretty much make anything. What the hell are you waiting for? A bell to ring? A fancy, engraved invitation? Get back in that damn kitchen, bitch!

●　●　●　●　●　●　●　●

GET BACK IN THE KITCHEN, *Bit@h!*

Entrées

Here we are again. You are ready to use what you've learned and make some amazing meals. As I said, this time around I have taken the recipes up a level. We are going to be using techniques and ingredients that we haven't used in the past to create recipes with more depth and more skill. Think you can handle it, bitch? Let's find out.

STUPID QUESTIONS... THAT WEREN'T TOO *Stupid*

Before we get started, I wanted to address some of your dumb-ass questions. I thought my direction in the previous book was unambiguous, but a number of you kept asking the same damn thing. So I thought I would clear a few things up.

You Say this Dish Requires Onions. What Kind of Onions Should I Use? This is just an example. You bitches also asked the same thing about vinegars, dry or sweet wines, and a plethora of other ingredients. So, here's the thing. When you cook with onions, they tend to lose a bit of their characterizing flavors. For example, the boldness of White, Red and Yellow onions will all tend to become sweet and mild when you apply heat to them. Whereas you can tell the difference between Red, White and Vidalia onions when they are raw, as you cook them, they all tend to revert to a sweet, onion-y, and mild flavor. Therefore, unless the recipe is calling for a specific type of onion, feel free to use whatever you have lying around the damn house.

Slightly different reasoning for vinegar and wine, but unless the recipe specifies a particular type, I have deemed that the flavor will work well with whichever you choose. So stop being such an anal bitch, damn it!

What's a "Pat of Butter"? I thought after the huge marketing effort in the 90's, that all of you would know what a freakin' pat of butter is. Turns out that I was uncharacteristically wrong. Well, the term goes way back to the old days when the bitches used to churn their own butter. A pat simply meant a small mass shaped by "patting." However, as we have progressed through the years, and modern miracles like refrigeration have allowed us to purchase our emulsified substances at the grocery store, the definition of a "pat" has changed. Today, when I talk about a "pat of butter," I am simply referring to a small square cut off the end of the stick. Basically, cut into the butter stick approximately a quarter inch to form one. If you are using a "tub," about a teaspoon will suffice.

What do You Mean By "Enough Olive Oil to Coat" When You Talk About Sautéing? Well, in this case, I would have accepted two interpretations. When I cook, I like to use only the amount of olive oil or other fat substance necessary to coat the vegetables that I am sautéing. This equates to about two tablespoons. I also would have been OK if you interpreted this to mean "enough olive oil or fatty substance to coat the bottom of the pan."

OK, now that that is out of the way, I think we might be ready to get our asses in the damn kitchen already. I have been working hard, testing recipes, and slaving away to come up with dishes that are worthy of you bitches. Again, I have also taken great pride in coming up with naughty names for your enjoyment. You better appreciate it damn it!

HAVE ANY MORE STUPID QUESTIONS, *Bit@h?*

LUSTY LAMB TOASTED *Ravioli*

(Lamb, Shallot and Portobello Stuffed Toasted Ravioli with a Creamy Tamarind Sauce)

RATING: ARE YOU F%@KING KIDDING *Me?*

Grocery List

Olive Oil

3 Shallots, diced fine

2 cloves of Garlic

2 medium sized Portabello Mushrooms diced fine

1 tsp Tamarind Paste

2 Lamb Chops finely cubed

1 cup Beef Broth

½ cup of Water

1 tbsp Cumin Powder

½ tbsp Paprika

1 Serrano Pepper seeded and finely chopped

½ tbsp Salt

½ tsp Ground Black Pepper

2 pats Butter

Flour

Refrigerated Pasta Dough (for Ravioli or Lasagna cut into squares)

2 Eggs

Bread Crumbs

Grated Parmesan Cheese

Flour

Vegetable Oil

¼ cup Heavy Cream

2 sprigs of Parsley chopped or 1 tsp Parsley Flakes

Preparation:

In a semi-deep, coverable frying pan, heat 2 tbsp of olive oil until hot. Add shallots and garlic and sauté for about 45 seconds until browned. Add portobello mushrooms and sauté for another minute or so. Lower heat to medium and add tamarind paste, cumin powder, paprika, serrano pepper, and lamb and brown for approximately 1- 2 minutes while stirring. Stir in beef broth and water and cover and bring to a boil for 20 seconds and then reduce heat to low and simmer for 10 mins.

In the meantime, coat pats of butter with flour and lay out your refrigerated pasta dough. After 10 mins of simmering, add the pats of butter to the sauce all the while stirring. Add 2 more tbsp of flour and stir to get most of the lumps out. Don't worry about all of the lumps, they will work out themselves while simmering. Cover and simmer for about 20 minutes more until sauce becomes thick. Stir occasionally so that the sauce doesn't stick to the bottom of the pan. Turn heat off and allow lamb to cool as you will be using it to fill pasta. Keep it covered.

If pasta has become too firm to work with, simply run it under some water to make it more pliable. If using fresh Lasagna pasta, cut it into squares about 4 inches long. If using ravioli pasta, simply use it as is. Stuff one side of the pasta with 1 tbsp of cool lamb mix (make sure to use all the lamb, as you will be using the sauce later). Fold pasta over, and pinch to seal like ravioli. (Again, if pasta doesn't seal, wet the edges with some water and pinch). Then lay out a bowl for flour and a bowl with the two eggs beaten, and one other bowl with a mixture of ¼ cup bread crumbs, ¼ cup flour, and ¼ cup of grated Parmesan cheese. Heat vegetable oil in deep pot for deep frying. You should only fill the oil up halfway in the pot. Coat pasta with flour, then egg, then bread crumb mixture and place (don't drop) into oil for approximately 1 minute or so until they become golden brown. Set aside on paper towels.

Reheat the sauce while stirring. Add heavy cream, and parsley until heated and blended smooth.

DRIZZLE SAUCE OVER RAVIOLI AND SERVE IT *Bit@h!*

WORDS OF *Wisdom*

Breading and deep frying ravioli creates an amazing texture and flavor.

Adding sour flavors like tamarind complements salty flavors.

Cream adds a rich taste to sauces.

Mild to hot peppers can really "open up" sauces.

S&M
(Sides & More)
Salad with your choice of homemade dressing
Steamed or sautéed green vegetable

YOU'RE A PIG! *Pasta*

(Baked Ziti in a Turkey, Tomato, and Bacon Bolgenese)

RATING: DUMB *Ass!*

Grocery List

½ Onion diced
Approximately 15 Grape Tomatoes sliced in half
4 Roma (Plum) Tomatoes cut into large chunks
2 cloves of Garlic chopped
Olive Oil
Salt
Ground Black Pepper
Paprika
Red Wine Vinegar
1 lb. Ground Turkey
3 strips of Bacon chopped
Can of Tomato Paste
Juice of half Lemon
¼ cup of Wine (Marsala or any Red)
½ lbs.-1 lb. of Ziti or Mastaccoli
Garlic Powder
Pinch of Crushed Red Pepper Flakes
Parsley Flakes
1 tbsp grated Parmesan Cheese
Fontina Cheese

Optional, But Recommended Vegetables

Diced Eggplant
Diced Mushrooms
Diced Celery
Diced Carrots
Diced Zucchini

In a coverable, deep, and large frying pan sauté onions, garlic tomatoes and any optional vegetables in enough olive oil to coat with a pinch of salt, pepper and paprika. Add tbsp of red wine vinegar. Sauté for approximately a minute until onions become translucent and garlic begins to brown. Then add turkey and bacon and brown while stirring everything together. You will notice that the turkey has a lot of water. This is OK, it will add volume to the sauce. Don't drain it bitch! Add tomato paste, lemon juice and wine and stir until paste loosens. Bring to point of bubbling and lower heat to "medium-low" and cover and simmer for at least 45 mins (For best results, let simmer for 1.5 to 2 hours) stirring occasionally. Add salt and pepper to taste, crushed red pepper, parsley flakes, some garlic powder, and grated Parmesan cheese. While sauce is simmering, freshly grate the Fontina cheese.

When the sauce is almost ready (about ten mins. before you decide to stop simmering) cook pasta according to directions, but for a minute less than suggested as you will be putting pasta in sauce. Toss pasta into pan with sauce and coat. Let simmer for about 1-2 minutes more.

Preheat oven to 325 degrees. Pour the pasta in a greased (with olive oil) baking or casserole dish. Sprinkle Fontina cheese on top along with ground black pepper, garlic powder and parsley flakes. Bake at 325 degrees for approximately 20 minutes (more if you like your pasta "toasted" or "crispy" which I do!) Make sure you check it every 15 minutes so you know its not burning.

DISH IT OUT AND SERVE IT *Bit@h!*

WORDS OF *Wisdom*

Wine complements tomatoes.

Bacon adds a smoky flavor to sauces and tastes awesome.

Adding different vegetables to tomato sauce makes it more robust.

Baking pasta isn't just for Lasagna.

Many of your favorite Italian dishes can become Baked Pasta dishes by using a little creativity.

Wine and lemon juice add tremendous flavor to tomato sauces.

S&M

(Sides & More)

Salad with Your Choice of Homemade Dressing

Steamed or Sautéed Green Vegetable

BÉSAME EL CULO *Cakes*

(Shrimp and Chorizo Cakes Served over Minty Mexican Corn Bread with a Cilantro and Garlic Remoulade)

RATING: DUMB *Ass!*

Grocery List

CHORIZO SHRIMP CAKES *Ingredients*

½ lb. Chorizo
½ pound of Shrimp peeled and de-tailed
½ tsp of Cumin
½ tsp of Paprika
½ tsp of Oregano
½ tsp of Chili powder
¼ cup Vinegar
Salt
¼ cup diced Jalapeño Peppers
¼ diced Onion
1 tbsp of Tomato Paste
3 cloves of Garlic diced
¼ cup of crushed Pineapple
¼ cup of fresh Cilantro chopped
Juice of 1 fresh Lime
1 Egg
1 heaping tsp of Flour
1 heaping tsp of Bread Crumbs
2 heaping tsp of Cornmeal
Vegetable Oil

CORN BREAD *Ingredients*

1 cup Butter, melted
½ cup Sugar
4 Eggs
1 cup of Corn
2 Jalapeño Peppers diced
¼ Onion diced
¼ cup of fresh Spearmint
¼ cup of Cilantro
½ cup shredded Cheddar Cheese
1 cup Flour
1 cup Cornmeal
4 teaspoons Baking Powder
¼ teaspoon Salt

CILANTRO MINT GARLIC *Remoulade*

½ cup of Cilantro
¼ cup of Mint
4 cloves of chopped Garlic
2 tbsp of Mayonnaise
Salt

CHORIZO SHRIMP *Cakes*

In a food processor, combine the chorizo, shrimp, cumin, paprika, oregano, chili powder, salt, jalapeño peppers, garlic, onion, tomato paste, pineapple, cilantro, spearmint, and lime juice. Pulse until shrimp is coarsely chopped. In a large mixing bowl, whisk egg. Add shrimp and chorizo mixture. Combine mixture with flour, bread crumbs, and corn meal and mix thoroughly until semi firm. Depending on the desired portion size, form the mixture into balls and flatten into cakes. Pan-fry in vegetable oil for 3-5 minutes per side.

MINTY MEXICAN *Corn Bread*

Preheat oven to 350 degrees and grease a 9x13 inch baking pan. In a large bowl, beat together butter and sugar. Beat in eggs one at a time. Blend in corn, chilies, onion, cilantro, mint and Cheddar cheese. In a separate bowl, stir together flour, corn meal, baking powder and salt. Add flour mixture to corn mixture; stir until smooth. Pour batter into prepared pan. Bake in preheated oven for 1 hour, until a toothpick inserted into center of the pan comes out clean.

CILANTRO MINT GARLIC *Remoulade*

In a food processor, combine all ingredients and mix thoroughly.

CUT A PIECE OF CORN BREAD, SPREAD REMOULADE ON TOP, AND PLACE
A CHORIZO SHRIMP CAKE OVER IT *Bit@h!*

WORDS OF *Wisdom*

Being creative with what you put into fried cakes can bring some unexpected and flavorful recipes.

Shrimp is complemented by the Mexican flavors in chorizo.

Pineapple juice really helps to bring Mexican flavors alive and provide a sweet combination.

S&M

(Sides & More)

Salad with Your Choice of Homemade Dressing

Steamed or Sautéed Green Vegetable

CARPE DIEM, *Bit@h?!?*

55

PETER, PETER, PUMPKIN *Pasta*
(Pasta with a Pumpkin Curry Bolgenese)

RATING: DUMB *Ass!*

Grocery List

½ Onion diced

4 cloves of Garlic chopped

Olive Oil

1 lb. ground Beef or Turkey

Sherry Cooking Wine

Apple Cider Vinegar

½ can of Pumpkin Purée (no sugar added, just pumpkin)

1 tbsp of Curry Powder

1 tsp of Chili Powder

½ tbsp of Cumin Powder

½ tbsp of Paprika

1 tbsp of Parsley Flakes

1 tbsp of Salt

½ tbsp of Ground Black Pepper

2 pats of Butter

1 lb (1 box) Penne Pasta

2 tbsp of grated Parmesan Cheese

S&M
(Sides & More)
Salad with Your Choice of Homemade Dressing

Steamed or Sautéed Green Vegetable

Preparation:

In a semi deep, coverable frying pan, sauté onion and garlic in enough olive oil to coat for approximately 1 min. until garlic begins to toast and onions become translucent. Add two swigs of sherry wine and 2 tbsp Apple Cider vinegar. Add ground meat and brown for approximately 1 minute more. Turn heat to medium. Add pumpkin purée and ¼ cup of sherry wine. Stir until it loosens and it becomes- sauce like. Add curry powder, chili powder, cumin, paprika, parsley flakes, salt and ground black pepper. Add pats of butter and 3 more tbsp of vinegar. Stir until consistent and smooth and bring heat to high until bubbling. Add grated Parmesan cheese and then turn heat to medium-low and cover to simmer for 20 minutes. Salt and pepper to taste.

While sauce is simmering, prepare pasta until it is half-way done.. approximately 5 minutes. Drain pasta and add to sauce until pasta is al dente- about 5 more minutes.

ADD EXTRA PARMESAN CHEESE AND SERVE IT, *Bit@h!*

WORDS OF *Wisdom*

Utilizing Pumpkin Purée in place of Tomato Paste can bring an unexpected flavor to dishes.
Curry complements the sweet taste of Pumpkin.
Chili Powder and Curry Powder are complementary spices.
Cooking pasta part-way in the sauce helps to let the flavors seep into the pasta.

LAY'ER DOWN *Lasagna*
(Taco Lasagna)

RATING: THE LITTLE CHEF THAT *Could!*

Grocery List

Olive Oil

1 lb ground Meat (Turkey, Pork or Beef)

3 cloves of Garlic chopped

3 Tomatoes diced

½ Onion diced

1 Carrot diced

2 Jalapeño or Serrano Peppers seeded and diced

4 tbsp Red Wine Vinegar

Ground Black Pepper

Salt

Paprika

¼ cup Orange Juice

¼ cup of Pineapple Juice

2 cans Tomato Paste

1 Lime

1 cup of frozen cut Corn

½ cup of Cilantro chopped

Chili Powder

Oregano

Cumin

Shredded Cheddar Cheese

Garlic Powder

Soft Corn Tortillas

SAUCE *Preparation:*

In a semi deep, coverable, frying pan, sauté garlic, onion and tomatoes with enough olive oil to coat and a sprinkle of salt for about a minute or until onions become translucent. Add ¼ tsp of cumin, ¼ tsp of paprika, ¼ tsp of chili powder and a little ground black pepper and sauté for another 30 seconds. Add vinegar, carrots, jalapeño or Serrano peppers, and sauté for another 30 seconds. Add ground meat and sauté for another minute until browned. Bring heat to medium and add orange and pineapple juice and stir thoroughly. Add tomato paste and stir till it loosens a bit. When it becomes a sauce-like consistency, add 1 tsp salt, 1 tbsp of cumin, 1 tbsp chili powder, 1 tbsp of garlic powder, ½ tsp of oregano, 1 tsp of paprika, juice of 1 lime, cilantro, and ground black pepper to taste. Mix thoroughly and raise heat to high. Wait until sauce starts to bubble, stir, and then bring to a simmer. Simmer for about 35 minutes. Add frozen corn and let sit for 1 minute.

LASAGNA *Preparation:*

Grease a semi-deep baking pan with olive oil on all sides. Put one layer of the corn tortilla on the bottom of the pan, followed by a layer of sauce, and then a layer of cheddar cheese. Repeat this step twice, so you have three layers of tortilla, sauce and cheese, making sure the last layer put down is the cheese. Sprinkle some garlic powder, paprika, parsley flakes, and pepper on the top, and bake for 20 minutes at 350 degrees.

LET COOL FOR ABOUT 5 MINUTES, THEN CUT INTO
PORTIONS AND SERVE IT, *Bit@h!*

WORDS OF *Wisdom*

Combining elements from two cuisines can produce an unexpected and flavorful meal.

Orange and Pineapple juices complement Mexican flavors really well and help to finish the dish.

S&M

(Sides & More)

Salad with Your Choice of Homemade Dressing
Steamed or Sautéed Green Vegetable

MEAT AND POTATOES *Mexicana*
(Mexican Shepherds Pie)

RATING: DUMB *Ass!*

Grocery List
Olive Oil
1 Onion diced
3 cloves of Garlic
2 Tomatoes diced
2 Jalapeño Peppers diced
1 Carrot diced
½ cup of Corn
Vinegar
1 lb. Ground Beef or Turkey
Chili Powder
Cumin
Oregano
Paprika
Juice of 1 Lime
2 tbsp Flour
2 Potatoes
Salt
Ground Black Pepper
Sour Cream
1 cup shredded Cheddar Cheese

NOTE TO THE *Bit@h!*

You will be using many of the ingredients in both parts of the recipe, so I suggest you read through the recipe so that you know which ones not to use all of. For example, you will be using one tomato for the first part of the recipe and one for the second step, so don't be a stupid bitch and use all of the tomatoes in the first part.

MEAT *Filling*

In a semi-deep frying pan, sauté 2 cloves garlic and ½ onion in enough olive oil to coat and a dash of salt and pepper for approximately a minute. Add 1 diced tomato, 1 of the diced jalapeño peppers, carrot, corn, 2 tbsp of vinegar, ½ tsp each of cumin, chili powder and paprika, and continue sautéing for another minute. Add the ground meat, 2 more tbsp of vinegar, juice of ½ lime, ½ tsp of chili powder, flour salt and pepper to taste and brown. Set aside.

POTATO *Topping*

Cut Potatoes in quarters and boil. When tender to the fork (approximately 15 minutes) remove from water and place in a bowl with 1 pat of butter, 2 tbsp of sour cream, rest of onion, jalapeño, garlic and tomato, ½ tsp each of cumin, paprika and chili powder, juice of the other half of lime and ½ cup of shredded cheddar cheese. Mash thoroughly.

ASSEMBLING THE *Pie*

In a semi-deep casserole dish, spread meat filling on the bottom. Place mashed potatoes on the top. Sprinkle the rest of the cheese on top and bake at 350 degrees for approximately 20 minutes until potatoes become crispy.

LET COOL FOR ABOUT 5 MINUTES, THEN CUT INTO
PORTIONS AND SERVE IT, *Bit@h!*

WORDS OF *Wisdom*

Blending culinary aspects of two cuisines can add unexpected flavor to dishes.

Meat and Potatoes always go together.

Potatoes are basically blank palettes for culinary flavor. Your favorite foods can be added to them.

S&M

(Sides & More)

Salad with Your Choice of Homemade Dressing

Steamed or Sautéed Green Vegetable

G-D SAVE THE *Bit@h!*

LICK ME! *Linguine*
(Linguine with a White Wine, Tomato and Bacon Sauce)

RATING: DUMB *Ass!*

Grocery List

Olive Oil

½ Onion diced

3 cloves Garlic diced

3 Roma (Plum) Tomatoes diced

½ tsp of Crushed Red Pepper

1 cup White Wine

1 cup of Chicken Broth

2 pats of Butter

3-4 strips of Bacon diced

Salt

Ground Black Pepper

Flour

1 lb. Linguine

Parmesan Cheese

2-3 sprigs Parsley or ½ tsp Parsley Flakes

S&M

(Sides & More)

Salad with Your Choice of Homemade Dressing

Steamed or Sautéed Green Vegetable

Preparation:

In a coverable, semi deep frying pan, sauté garlic and onion in enough olive oil to coat with a dash of salt and pepper for 1-2 minutes until the onions become translucent. Add tomatoes and bacon and ½ tsp of crushed red pepper and continue to sauté for another minute or so. Cover pan and let sit for about 2 minutes until tomatoes start to get tender. Uncover and begin to squish tomatoes with the back of a spoon. Add cup of white wine' cup of chicken broth, 2 pats of butter, ½ tsp of salt, ½ tsp pepper, stir and cover. Let simmer for about 10 minutes or so. Add 2 tbsp of flour and stir to get most of the lumps out. Don't worry about all the lumps, just get the big ones, the other ones will work their way out naturally. Cover and simmer for another 15-20 minutes while you make pasta. Make sure to stir it occasionally so it doesn't stick to bottom of pan.

Prepare linguine according to directions. When drained, add pasta and parsley directly to sauce and toss for a minute or so.

ADD PARMESAN CHEESE AND
SERVE IT, *Bit@h!*

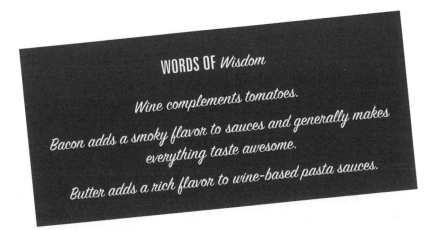

WORDS OF *Wisdom*

Wine complements tomatoes.

Bacon adds a smoky flavor to sauces and generally makes everything taste awesome.

Butter adds a rich flavor to wine-based pasta sauces.

KNOCK ME UP! *Noodles*
(Pork and Shrimp Fried Ramen)

RATING: DUMB *Ass!*

Grocery List

Sesame Oil

½ Onion diced

3 cloves Garlic diced

3 Carrots diced

½ cup frozen Corn

1 Pork Shoulder Blade Steak cubed finely

Soy Sauce

Vinegar

Cumin

Paprika

Ground Black Pepper

2 packages Ramen Noodles

1 cup frozen Shrimp

½ cup frozen Peas

1 Egg beaten

S&M
(Sides & More)
Sun dried Tomato, Caper and Parmesan Gyoza

Salad with your choice of homemade dressing

Preparation:

In a coverable wok or deep frying pan, sauté onion and garlic in enough sesame oil to coat for 1-2 minutes until onions become translucent. Add carrots and corn and sauté for an additional two minutes. Add pork, 1 tbsp soy sauce, 1 tbsp of vinegar, ½ tsp each of cumin, paprika, and ground black pepper and continue to sauté for another minute or two. Add ¼ cup of water, 3 tbsp of soy sauce and 3 tbsp of vinegar. Set heat to medium low, stir and cover. Let simmer for approximately 15 minutes. Crush Ramen noodles thoroughly so they are broken up into small bits. Place Ramen in pan and stir to immerse in liquid. If you need to, you can add a little more water. Cover and let sit for about 5 minutes so the ramen absorbs liquid and gets soft. Add shrimp and peas and stir. Cover and let sit about 2 minutes so peas and shrimp defrost. Make a hole in the ramen/vegetable/pork mix in the center so you can see the bottom of the pan. Make sure pan is on medium low heat and pour the beaten egg in the center. Let the egg sit for about 1 minute until it starts to harden. When it starts to harden, but still has a "loose" consistency, mix it thoroughly in with the rest of the ramen/vegetable/pork/shrimp mix. Keep mixing until all of the egg is cooked. Finish off with a splash of soy sauce and mix in, if you desire.

SERVE IT, *Bit@h!*

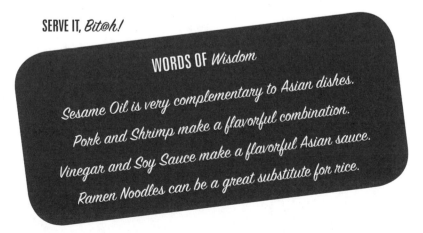

WORDS OF *Wisdom*

Sesame Oil is very complementary to Asian dishes.

Pork and Shrimp make a flavorful combination.

Vinegar and Soy Sauce make a flavorful Asian sauce.

Ramen Noodles can be a great substitute for rice.

CHILL OUT CHUMP! *Chicken*

(Chicken Rollatini with Sun Dried Tomatoes, Capers and Parmesan in a Marsala Wine Sauce)

RATING: ARE YOU F%@KING KIDDING *Me?*

Grocery List

4 Chicken Breasts

1 Egg beaten

3 tbsp of Flour

3 tbsp of Bread Crumbs

Olive Oil

½ Onion diced

3 cloves Garlic diced

½ cup of Sun Dried Tomatoes

2 tbsp Capers

Parmesan Cheese

Marsala Wine

¼ cup Beef Broth

½ cup of Water

Salt

Ground Black Pepper

1 pat of Butter

1 pat of Butter coated with Flour

NOTE TO THE *Bit@h!*

You will be using half of the onion, garlic and sun dried tomatoes in the first step, and half in the second part of the recipe, so plan accordingly, bitch. Don't f%@k it up!

CHICKEN *Preparation*

Carefully slice the chicken breasts in half the LONG way (butterfly-cut) so there are two thin pieces of poultry. For example, place the chicken breast flat on the counter. Make sure the blade of the knife is parallel to the counter and starting at one end cut through the entire breast making two thin chicken breasts. With a meat tenderizer, you can pound the chicken into thinner strips if you want. (I suggest you want.)

ROLLATINI *Filling*

In a blender, combine 1 cup sun dried tomatoes, 1-2 tbsps Parmesan cheese, 1-2 tsp capers, 1 clove garlic and ¼ onion, 2 tbsp of Olive Oil, ½ tsp of ground black pepper. Pulse thoroughly until it turns into a paste.

ASSEMBLY
(You will need toothpicks or butcher string for this step)

Spread the sun dried filling in a thin layer on one side of each of the chicken breast slices. Starting from one side, roll the thin breasts tightly. Fasten with the toothpicks or the butcher's string and set aside.

Beat the egg and put in a bowl. Combine the flour and the bread crumbs. If you want (and I suggest you want to) sprinkle a little (1 tsp each) garlic powder, black pepper, and Parmesan cheese into the mixture. Then dip and roll chicken into the dry mixture, then the egg, then the dry mixture again and set aside.

In a semi-deep, coverable frying pan, heat about a quarter of an inch thick olive oil to coat the pan over medium high heat. When oil is hot, place the chicken rolls in the pan and brown on all sides. While browning, add a few swigs of Marsala wine, leave chicken in for approximately three minutes to begin the cooking process while making sure to periodically roll the chicken. Then take out and set aside.

In the same pan, add a few swigs of Marsala wine to deglaze. Add rest of garlic and onions, sun dried tomato, and capers and sauté for a minute or so. Add chicken broth, water, ¼ cup more Marsala wine, ½ tsp of pepper. Add 1 (non-flour coated) pat of butter and bring to a boil for a minute and then simmer. Place chicken back in sauce and cover and simmer for 20-25 minutes. Take chicken out and cover to keep warm. Add 1 pat of flour coated butter and an additional 1 tbsp of flour and ½ tsp of Parmesan cheese and stir to thicken sauce. Stir to get most of the lumps out. Don't worry about all the lumps, just get the big ones, the other ones will work their way out naturally. Cover and simmer for another 15-20 minutes. Make sure to stir it occasionally so it doesn't stick to bottom of pan. Cut strings on chicken or remove the toothpicks. If the chicken has become too cold, place back in the sauce for 2-3 minutes. Then remove and drizzle the sauce over the rolls.

DRIZZLE SAUCE OVER ROLLS
AND SERVE IT, *Bit@h!*

●　●　●　●　●　●

The Marsala wine really helps to tame the salty flavor of the Capers and Parmesan while complementing the Tomatoes. Breading Chicken helps to retain its moisture. Simmering the Chicken helps to enhance its flavor.

S&M

(Sides & More)

Sun dried Tomato, Caper and Parmesan Gyoza

Salad with your choice of homemade dressing

Sautéed or steamed green vegetable

WHO'S THE HUNTER NOW, *Bit@h?!?*

BRAISE MY BUTT! *Lamb*

(Braised Lamb Shank with a Red Wine, Peppercorn and Cream Sauce)

RATING: DUMB *Ass!*

Grocery List

Lamb Shank

1-2 cups of Red Wine (your choice)

4 tbsp Worcestershire Sauce

2 tsp freshly Ground Black Peppercorns

1 tsp Salt

Olive Oil

3 cloves of Garlic crushed

½ Onion finely diced

1 cup of Beef Broth

2 Bay Leaves

Flour

¼ cup Heavy Cream

2 pats of Butter

S&M

(Sides & More)

Sun Dried Tomato, Caper and Parmesan Gyoza

Salad with your choice of homemade dressing

Sautéed or steamed green vegetable

Deep-Fried Sweet Potato and Jalapeño Balls

Mexican Mashed Potatoes

Scalloped Potatoes with Horseradish Mustard and Sour Cream

MARINADE

Combine red wine, freshly ground peppercorns, Worcestershire sauce, and mix thoroughly. Marinate lamb shank for minimum of 3 hours, but preferably overnight.

PREPARATION

Separate lamb from marinade and set aside. In a semi-deep, coverable pan, sauté onion and garlic in enough olive oil to coat for one minute. Gently brown the lamb on all sides for about a minute or so, enough to simply sear the meat. Pour beef broth in the pan. Pour marinade into pan until it is half way to three quarters of the way up the meat and bring to a boil for 30 seconds to one minute then lower heat to simmer. Put in a bay leaves, tsp of salt, cover and cook for 3-4 hours.

After 3-4 hours take Lamb out carefully as it will most likely fall off the bone. Cover it to keep warm. Add butter, cream and 2 tbsp of flour to remaining broth and continuously stir to thicken sauce. Let simmer for about 10-15 minutes. Once thickened to a sauce-like consistency (soupy is too little, and gravy is to thick), salt to taste.

**DRIZZLE SAUCE OVER LAMB
AND SERVE IT, *Bit@h!***

WORDS OF *Wisdom*

Braising Lamb Shanks and other tough meats help to make them very tender.

Cream adds a rich flavor to wine based sauces.

Red Wine adds a deep flavor to meats.

Ground Black Pepper complements cream based sauces.

MUNCH ON MY MEAT! *Marsala*
(Braised Ribs with a Marsala, Tomato Cream Sauce)

RATING: DUMB *Ass!*

Grocery List

Olive Oil
½ Onion Diced
3 cloves of Garlic diced
Beef or Pork Ribs
1 cup, Marsala wine
1 cup Chicken Broth
4 Roma (plum) Tomatoes diced
Salt
Ground Black Pepper
2 Bay Leaves
2 springs of fresh Parsley chopped
2 pats of Butter
½ cup Heavy Cream
Flour

S&M

(Sides & More)

Sun Dried Tomato, Caper and Parmesan Gyoza

Salad with your choice of homemade dressing

Sautéed or steamed green vegetable

Deep-Fried Sweet Potato and Jalapeño Balls

Mexican Mashed Potatoes

Scalloped Potatoes with Horseradish Mustard and Sour Cream

Preparation:

In a semi-deep, coverable pan, sauté onion and garlic in enough olive oil to coat for one minute. Gently brown the ribs on all sides for one to two minutes, enough to simply sear the meat. Then set aside. Pour a swig of Marsala wine in the pan to deglaze and then add a about a teaspoon of olive oil and the tomatoes. Sauté for two to three minutes until tomatoes become tender. Add Marsala wine, chicken broth, 1 tsp of pepper, 1 tsp of salt, and bring to a boil for 30 seconds to one minute then lower heat to simmer. When sauce is simmering, place ribs into mixture, and add bay leaves. Cover and simmer for 3-4 hours. By the end, a lot of the liquid may have evaporated and you will be left with chunks of tomatoes, garlic and onion in a sauce like consistency.

After 3-4 Hours take ribs out carefully as they will most likely fall off the bone. If there is still a liquid consistency to the sauce, add a little flour to thicken it a bit. Add parsley, butter and cream and stir for a minute.

DRIZZLE SAUCE OVER RIBS OR PROVIDE AS A DIPPING SAUCES
AND SERVE 'EM UP *Bit@h!*

WORDS OF *Wisdom*

Braising Ribs and other tough meats help to make them very tender.

Cream adds a rich flavor to wine and Tomato-based sauces. Marsala and other darker wines add a heartier flavor to dishes.

DON'T CALL ME CHICKEN, *Bit@h!*
(Chicken in a Marsala Dijon Sauce)

RATING: THE LITTLE CHEF THAT *Could!*

Grocery List

Flour
Bread Crumbs
Garlic Powder
Onion Powder
Parsley Flakes
Salt
Ground Black Pepper
1 Egg
Parmesan Cheese
2-4 Chicken Breasts
½ Onion diced
3 cloves Garlic diced
¼ cup Marsala Wine
1 cup Beef Broth
¼ cup of Dijon Mustard
2 pats of Butter

Preparation:

Mix ½ cup flour with ¼ cup bread crumbs, 1 tbsp garlic powder, 1 tbsp onion powder, 1 tbsp parsley flakes, 1 tsp of pepper and a pinch of salt. Crack 1 egg in separate bowl and beat. Prepare chicken pieces by dipping in flour mixture, then covering in egg and then dredging in flour mixture again. Set aside.

In a semi-deep, coverable frying pan, sauté onion and garlic with enough olive oil to coat. Add salt and pepper to taste. Sauté for 1 minute. Add enough Marsala wine to cover bottom of pan. Brown chicken on either side for 30 seconds to one minute until flour mixture is cooked through and adheres to chicken. Take out and set aside.

In same pan, add more Marsala wine to deglaze the pan. Add beef broth, ¼ cup Marsala wine, butter, Dijon mustard, 1 tbsp of garlic powder, 1 tbsp of Onion Powder, 1 tbsp Parsley Flakes, ½ tsp of pepper, pinch of salt (remember most beef broth has a lot of salt, so be gentle). Bring to a boil, then simmer. Add chicken (only when it has stopped boiling, no sooner) Cover and simmer for 30 mins.

Take chicken out and set aside. Using the broth/Marsala mixture slowly stir in 2 tbsp of flour to thicken sauce. Stir until fairly smooth, try to get all lumps out. Simmer for approximately 10-15 minutes more to allow tho thicken. Finish of with a little fresh parsley or parsley flakes about a minute before serving. You can put chicken back in sauce about 2 minutes before serving to warm it.

DRIZZLE SAUCE ON TOP OF CHICKEN AND SERVE IT, *Bit@h!*

WORDS OF *Wisdom*

Marsala Wine and Mustard combine to make a great base for flavor.

Breading Chicken helps to retain moisture.

Flour helps to thicken pan juices to make into sauce or gravy.

S&M

(Sides & More)

Salad with your choice of homemade dressing

Scalloped Potatoes with Horseradish Mustard and Sour Cream

Asparagus and Shiitake Custard

Sautéed or steamed green vegetable

TAJ MAHAL *Meatloaf*
(Curry Mustard Meatloaf)

RATING: DUMB *Ass!*

Grocery List
1 lb. of Ground Turkey or Chicken (can use beef, but I find the poultry more appealing for this dish)
½ Onion diced
1-2 Garlic cloves chopped
1 Baking Potato
½ cup Dijon Mustard
Curry Powder
Chili Powder
1 Egg
Bread Crumbs
Salt
Ground Black Pepper
Olive Oil

Preparation:

Preheat oven to 375 degrees.

Grate the potato into thin strings in a strainer and squeeze out the excess water. Place in a bowl. In same bowl, combine ground meat, onion, garlic, Dijon mustard, 1 tbsp of curry powder, 1 tbsp of chili powder, egg, ½ cup of bread crumbs, 1-2 tsp salt, 1 tsp ground black pepper, and 1 tbsp olive oil. Mix thoroughly until even.

Place meat mixture into greased (oiled) baking pan. Bake for 50-60 minutes checking periodically towards the end to make sure it does not burn.

CUT AND SERVE IT, *Bit@h!*

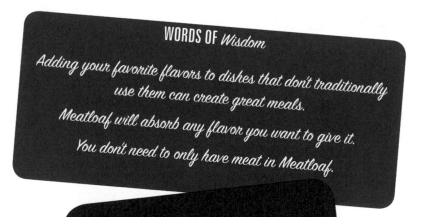

WORDS OF *Wisdom*

Adding your favorite flavors to dishes that don't traditionally use them can create great meals.

Meatloaf will absorb any flavor you want to give it.

You don't need to only have meat in Meatloaf.

S&M

(Sides & More)

Salad with your choice of homemade dressing

Deep-Fried Sweet Potato and Jalapeño Balls

Asparagus and Shiitake Custard

Sautéed or steamed green vegetable

MOTHER CLUCKER *Meatloaf*
(Mexican Meatloaf)

RATING: DUMB *Ass!*

Grocery List

1 lb. of Ground Beef, Pork, Turkey or Chicken
½ large Onion diced
3 Garlic cloves chopped
2 Jalapeño Peppers seeded and diced
½ cup of frozen Corn
1 Tomato diced
1 Lime
Cumin Powder
Chili Powder
Paprika
3 tbsp Tomato Paste
1 Egg
Bread Crumbs
Salt
Ground Black Pepper
Olive Oil

Preparation:

Preheat oven to 375 degrees

Dice tomato and set on paper towels to thoroughly drain the excess water. In a bowl, combine ground meat, onion, garlic, jalapeños, corn, tomatoes, juice of half a lime, 1 tbsp of cumin powder, 1 tbsp of chili powder, 1 tbsp of paprika, tomato paste, egg, 1 cup of bread crumbs, 1 tsp salt, ½ tsp ground black pepper, and one tbsp olive oil. Mix thoroughly until even.

Place meat mixture into greased (oiled) baking pan. Bake for 50-60 minutes checking periodically towards the end to make sure it does not burn.

CUT AND SERVE IT, *Bit@h!*

WORDS OF *Wisdom*

Adding your favorite flavors to dishes that don't traditionally use them can create great meals.

Meatloaf will absorb any flavor you want to give it.

You don't need to only have meat in Meatloaf.

S&M

(Sides & More)

Salad with your choice of homemade dressing

Deep-Fried Sweet Potato and Jalapeño Balls

Mexican Mashed Potatoes

Mexican Mashed Potato Spheres

SPAGHETTI AND *Meatloaf*
(Meatloaf with Spaghetti and Tomato Sauce)

RATING: DUMB *Ass!*

Grocery List
INGREDIENTS FOR TOMATO *Sauce*
½ Onion diced
4 cloves Garlic chopped
2 Roma Tomatoes diced
10-15 Grape Tomatoes halved
1 can Tomato Paste
½ cup Red or Marsala Wine
Juice of 1 Lemon
½ tsp of Sugar
Salt
Ground Black Pepper
Crushed Red Pepper flakes
3 tbsp Parmesan Cheese
¼ cup of fresh Parsley or Parsley flakes

INGREDIENTS FOR *Meatloaf*
1 lb. of Ground Beef or Turkey
1 cup of Bread Crumbs
¼ lb. of cooled, cooked Spaghetti
1 tsp Salt
1 Egg
Shredded Fontina Cheese
Garlic Powder
Ground Black Pepper
2 sprigs of Parsley chopped or 1 tsp of Parsley Flakes

Preparation:

TOMATO *Sauce*

Sauté onion and garlic in enough olive oil to coat with dash salt and pepper for about a minute. Add Roma tomatoes and grape tomatoes and sauté on medium- medium high heat for another two minutes until tomatoes start to "melt" or break down. I like to mash them a bit at this point so the fibers start to become sauce-like. Add just enough wine to deglaze pot and stir. Add tomato paste and begin to stir until it becomes "sauce-like". Add ½ cup of wine, lemon Juice (can substitute 3 tbsp of vinegar here) and sugar and stir until everything becomes consistent. Add salt and pepper to taste, a few sprinkles of crushed red pepper, and Parmesan cheese. Cover, set heat to medium low and simmer for about 45 minutes to an hour, stirring occasionally. About 10 minutes before finishing, add the parsley or parsley flakes, and stir. Let cool and set aside.

PREPARATION FOR *Meatloaf*

Preheat oven to 375 degrees.

In a bowl combine ground meat, bread crumbs, spaghetti salt and 1 cup of the sauce you just made and mix thoroughly. Then add egg and mix thoroughly.

Put in a greased baking pan. Spread more sauce on top of meat and put in oven for 40 minutes. Take out and grate Fontina cheese on top. Sprinkle garlic powder, ground black pepper and parsley on top. Bake for an additional 15 minutes until cheese is melted.

CUT AND SERVE IT, *Bit@h!*

WORDS OF *Wisdom*

Adding your favorite flavors to dishes that don't traditionally use them can create great meals.

Meatloaf will absorb any flavor you want to give it.

You don't need to only have meat in Meatloaf.

S&M

(Sides & More)

Salad with your choice of homemade dressing

Steamed or sautéed green vegetable

IT'S FUN TO COOK AT THE Y-M-C-A, *Bit@h!*

ARTI-CHOKE THE *Chicken*
(Chicken with White Whine, Capers and Artichokes)

RATING: THE LITTLE CHEF THAT *Could!*

Grocery List

Chicken Legs and Thighs (can use breasts if you don't like dark meat, but I find it works the best for this dish)

Olive Oil

½ cup Capers with vinegar in jar

White Wine

½ cup of Chicken Broth

Ground Black Pepper

Oregano

½ Onion diced

3 cloves Garlic diced

½ cup of Olives sliced

1 cup of Artichoke Hearts quartered

2 pats of Butter

Flour

S&M

(Sides & More)

Salad with your choice of homemade dressing

Steamed or sautéed green vegetable

MARINADE

Combine capers (with vinegar it came in) and a half bottle of white wine and chicken broth with three tbsp of olive oil and ½ tsp of ground black pepper and tsp of oregano. Mix thoroughly and put chicken in for at least two hours.

Optional: When you are ready to cook, you can lightly flour the chicken, but this is not necessary. If you lightly flour, it will give a nice crust around the chicken when you brown it in the next step.

PREPARATION

In a deep frying pan, sauté onion and garlic in enough olive oil to coat for about a minute. Then brown each piece of chicken on all sides. Pour rest of marinade on top so that it covers ¾ of the way up the chicken pieces. If you don't have enough of the marinade left to cover ¾ of the way up, you can add a little more chicken broth. Add olives, artichoke hearts and butter. Cover and let simmer for 40 minutes until chicken is cooked through. (Will have to cut to the bone to make sure.) Take the chicken out. Add 1-2 tbsp of flour to thicken sauce. Stir to get most of the lumps out. Focus on the big lumps as the others will smooth out naturally. Cover and simmer for approximately 10-15 minutes to allow sauce to thicken. Stir occasionally to avoid sauce sticking to bottom of pan.

DRIZZLE SAUCE OVER CHICKEN OR SERVE IT IN A "DIPPING DISH" ON THE SIDE, *Bit@h!*

WORDS OF *Wisdom*

White Wine and Butter can be combined to add a rich, yet light flavor to sauces.

Vinegar from the Capers complements salty flavors.

Oregano can really bring depth to certain cuisines, but use it sparingly as it will take over the dish.

THAI ME DOWN *Chicken*
(Thai Chicken with Basmati Rice)

RATING: DUMB *Ass!*

S&M

(Sides & More)

Coconut Shrimp Balls

Salad with your choice of homemade dressing

Preparation:

In a coverable wok or deep frying pan, sauté onion and garlic in enough sesame oil to coat (approximately 2 tbsp) for 1-2 minutes until onions become translucent. Add chicken, lemongrass, 1 tbsp of peanut sauce, 1 tbsp soy sauce, 1 tbsp of vinegar, ½ tsp each of cumin, paprika, and ground black pepper and continue to sauté for another minute or two. Add ¾ cup of water, 2 more tbsp of peanut sauce, 2-3 tbsp of soy sauce and 3 tbsp of vinegar, ½ tsp more of cumin and paprika. Add a good sprinkle of red chili powder (remember this stuff is potent, so only add a good sprinkle.) Set heat to medium low, stir, and cover. Let simmer for approximately 25-30 minutes.

While simmering, you can prepare rice or can prepare rice beforehand. Typical rice preparation calls for 1 cup of rice to 2 cups of water. Bring to a boil, cover and simmer for 10-20 minutes until all water is absorbed.

When rice is done, combine it with chicken mixture and stir thoroughly until all rice is drenched in sauce. Let rice sit in sauce for about 2-3 minutes and stir.

SERVE IT, *Bit@h!*

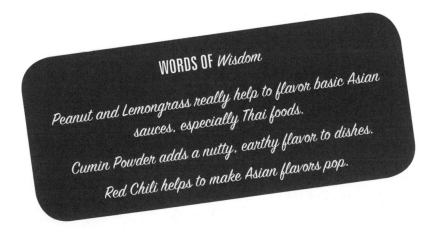

WORDS OF *Wisdom*

Peanut and Lemongrass really help to flavor basic Asian sauces, especially Thai foods.

Cumin Powder adds a nutty, earthy flavor to dishes.

Red Chili helps to make Asian flavors pop.

PIMP ME OUT! *Pasta*
(Chicken Parmigiana Pasta)

RATING: THE LITTLE CHEF THAT *Could!*

Grocery List

Chicken cut into strips (2-4 breasts)
White or Marsala Wine (Marsala gives a deeper flavor)
1 Egg
Flour
Garlic Powder
Onion Powder
Parsley Flakes
Salt
Ground Black Pepper
Olive Oil
½ Onion
1 clove Garlic
Fontina Cheese
Penne, Ziti or Rigatoni

INGREDIENTS FOR TOMATO *Sauce*
4 cloves Garlic chopped
5 Roma (Plum) Tomatoes diced
10-15 Grape Tomatoes halved
1 can Tomato Paste
½ cup Wine (Red, White or Marsala- You choose)
Juice of 1 Lemon
½ tsp of Sugar
Salt
Ground Black Pepper
Crushed Red Pepper Flakes
3 tbsp Parmesan Cheese
¼ cup of fresh Parsley or Parsley Flakes

Preparation:

Mix ½ cup flour with 2 tbsps Parmesan cheese, 1 tbsp garlic powder, 1 tbsp onion powder, 1 tbsp parsley flakes, 1 tbsp of pepper and a pinch of salt. Crack 1 egg in separate bowl and beat with 1 tsp Parmesan cheese, 1 tsp parsley flakes, 1 tsp pepper and a pinch of salt. Prepare chicken pieces by covering flour mixture, then in egg mixture and then dredging in flour mixture again. Set aside.

In a semi-deep, coverable frying pan, chop onion and 1 clove of garlic and sauté with enough olive oil to coat. Add pinch of salt and pepper. Sauté for 1 minute. Add enough white or Marsala wine to cover bottom of pan. Brown chicken on either side for 30 seconds to one minute until flour mixture is cooked through and adheres to chicken. Take out and set aside.

TOMATO *Sauce*

In the same pan, sauté additional garlic (from sauce ingredients) in enough olive oil to coat with dash salt and pepper for about a minute. Add Roma tomatoes and grape tomatoes, cover and let sit on medium-medium high heat for another two minutes until tomatoes start to "melt" or break down. I like to mash them a bit at this point so the fibers start to become sauce-like. Add a swig of wine (red, white or Marsala) to deglaze pot and stir. Add tomato paste and begin to stir until it becomes "sauce-like." Add ½ cup of wine, lemon juice (can substitute 3 tbsp of vinegar here) and sugar and stir until everything becomes consistent. Add salt and pepper to taste and a few sprinkles of crushed red pepper, and Parmesan cheese. Cover, set heat to medium low and simmer for about 45 minutes to an hour, stirring occasionally. About 10 minutes before finishing, add the parsley or parsley flakes, and stir. Add back chicken pieces and let simmer for 10 minutes.

While sauce is simmering, make pasta according to directions on package, and shred Fontina cheese.

ASSEMBLY AND *Baking*

Set oven to 350 degrees. In a casserole dish, mix pasta, sauce and chicken. Top with shredded cheese, and a dash each of parsley flakes, garlic powder, and ground black pepper. Bake for 15-20 minutes.

DISH IT OUT AND SERVE IT, *Bit@h!*

WORDS OF *Wisdom*

Baking pasta isn't just for Lasagna. Many of your favorite Italian dishes can become baked pasta dishes by adding a layer of Italian cheeses. Wine and Lemon Juice add tremendous flavor to tomato sauces.

S&M

(Sides & More)

Salad with your choice of homemade dressing
Steamed or sautéed green vegetable

BREAK MY *Chops*
(Pan Roasted Lamb or Pork Chops with a Mango Cumin Salsa)

RATING: THE LITTLE CHEF THAT *Could!*

Grocery List

Olive Oil
½ Onion diced
1 Jalapeño Pepper diced
3 Garlic cloves chopped
2 Tomatoes diced
1 Mango diced finely
5 sprigs of Cilantro chopped
White Wine
Juice of half a Lemon
Salt
Ground Black Pepper
Cumin
2-4 Lamb or Pork Chops (depending on how many people)

ET TU, *Bit@h?!?*

Preparation:

Season Lamb or Pork with salt, pepper and cumin and set aside.

Preheat oven to 350 degrees.

In a semi deep, oven safe, frying pan, sauté garlic onions, and jalapeño in enough oil to coat, approximately 2 tbsp, for about a minute. Add pinch of salt and ground black pepper, 1 tbsp of Cumin and a few swigs of white wine and sauté for about two more minutes. Add diced tomatoes, mangos, and cilantro and heat for 1 more minute. (Enough time to gently heat the tomatoes and mangos.) Place all of the vegetables in a bowl and set aside. Cover and allow to come to room temperature.

While vegetables are cooling, add a enough olive oil to coat the pan, and bring heat to medium. When olive oil is heated again, (test to make sure it is thoroughly heated by placing a corner of the chop into the oil. If it sizzles immediately, then it is hot enough) place the lamb or pork into the pan for about 2 minutes per side.

Then place pan with meat directly into the oven for 8-10 minutes. While meat is heating, add lemon juice to salsa and stir. Salt and pepper to taste

WHEN MEAT IS READY, PLACE A FEW SCOOPS
OF SALSA ON TOP AND SERVE IT, *Bit@h!*

WORDS OF *Wisdom*

Pan-Roasting can be a great way to prepare thicker cuts of meat quickly.

Citrus combines with cumin to give a light, nutty flavor which can be a perfect flavoring for vegetables and meats.

Adding a chunky salsa to meats can really help to bring texture as well as flavor to a dish.

S&M

(Sides & More)

Mexican Mashed Potatoes
Mexican Mashed Potato Spheres
Deep-Fried Sweet Potato Jalapeño Balls
Scalloped Potatoes with Horseradish Mustard and Sour Cream
Steamed or sautéed vegetable of your choosing

SCREW PROHIBITION, *Bit@h?!?*

HERE'S THE BEEF *Pasta*

(Pasta with Beef, Capers, and Sun Dried Tomatoes in a Marsala Wine Sauce)

RATING: THE LITTLE CHEF THAT *Could!*

Grocery List

½ lb. Beef cubed (your choice of meat- see instructions)

2 cloves Garlic chopped

½ Onion diced

2 tbsp Capers

¼ cup of Sun Dried Tomatoes chopped

Ground Black Pepper

1 cup of Beef Broth

½ cup of Marsala Wine

2 pats of Butter

1 lb. of Penne or Rigatoni Pasta

1 tbsp Parmesan Cheese

2 tbsp Flour

CHOICE OF *Beef*

Your choice of beef will alter this recipe. If you choose a tougher cut of meat like brisket or chuck, you will need to marinate the beef in a mixture of Marsala wine and capers overnight. You will also need to first brown and sear it and then simmer this beef in the marinade for about 2 hours prior to making the recipe as well. This will serve to make the beef more tender.

If you choose a quick frying beef such as a ribeye or specific stir-fry beef (ask about it at the grocery store) you will just need to quickly sauté it and set it aside until the end of the recipe.

Preparation:

In a semi deep frying pan, sauté garlic and onions in enough olive oil to coat for approximately 1 minute until onions become translucent. Add sun dried tomatoes and capers and sauté for another 30 seconds or so. Add beef, pinch of pepper, and brown. (approximately 1-2 minutes). If you are using the less tough cuts of meat, remove the meat and set aside at this point. If you are using the already simmered tougher beef, keep it in the pot for the rest of this recipe. Add 1 cup beef broth, 1 cup Marsala wine and ½ tsp of pepper. Add butter and bring to a boil for a minute and then turn heat to low/medium-low and simmer for approximately 10 minutes. Add 2 tbsp of flour and stir to get the larger lumps out. Then simmer for about 15-20 minutes more occasionally stirring so the sauce doesn't stick to the bottom of the pan.

While simmering, prepare pasta according to directions. Once finished, set aside and pour a tbsp of olive oil and mix so it doesn't stick together.

Approximately 5 minutes before you are done simmering, you should add back the beef that you sautéed before (if you used the less tough cuts of meat). Approximately two minutes before simmering of sauce is done, add Parmesan cheese. Add pasta to sauce and allow to heat through for a minute or so.

SERVE IT, *Bit@h!*

WORDS OF *Wisdom*

Marsala wine adds a robust, not fruity flavor to dishes

Butter adds a rich flavor to pasta sauces.

Capers can bring a tangy flavor to a dish as a result of the Vinegar it is packed in, and complements salty flavors.

Parmesan Cheese complements most wine and Tomato-based sauces.

S&M

(Sides & More)

Salad with your choice of homemade dressing
Steamed or sautéed green vegetable

BITCHIN' *Burrito*
(Shrimp Burrito Pie)

RATING: DUMB *Ass!*

Grocery List

Olive Oil

½ Onion diced

2 cloves Garlic diced

2 cups of frozen Shrimp thawed and de-tailed

1 Jalapeño Pepper diced

2 Tomato diced

½ tsp Cumin powder

½ tsp Chili powder

½ tsp Salt

½ tsp Ground Black Pepper

½ tsp Paprika

Juice of ½ Lime

3-5 sprigs of fresh Cilantro chopped

½ cup of shredded Pepper Jack Cheese

1 can of Tomato Sauce

Flour Tortillas

Preparation:

In a semi deep frying pan, sauté garlic and onions in enough olive oil to coat for approximately 1 minute until onions become translucent, then add shrimp, tomatoes, jalapeño pepper, cumin powder, chili powder, salt, pepper, and paprika, stir, and sauté for another 30 seconds or so. Add lime juice, cilantro and sauté for another 2-3 minutes on medium low heat. Drain excess liquid into a pot, add the tomato sauce, then cover and place on stove at a low to medium low setting. Set aside shrimp and vegetables.

Pre heat oven to 350 degrees. Grease a 9 inch x 9 inch baking pan with olive oil and line bottom with flour tortillas. Then shrimp filling, then add half of the pepper jack cheese. Top with another layer of tortillas and brush some olive oil on the top. Then add the rest of pepper jack cheese. Sprinkle with garlic powder and pepper and bake for approximately 10 minutes until cheese is melted.

CUT IT CAREFULLY INTO SQUARE PORTIONS. DRIZZLE SOME
OF THE SAUCE ON TOP AND SERVE IT, *Bit@h!*

WORDS OF *Wisdom*

Shrimp is complemented by Mexican flavors.
Preparing your favorite dishes in a different fashion can make unexpected and great meals.

S&M

(Sides & More)
Salad with your choice of homemade dressing
Steamed or sautéed green vegetable

HOLY SH!T *Ravioli*

(Chicken Ravioli in a White Wine and Saffron Cream Sauce)

RATING: THE LITTLE CHEF THAT *Could!*

Grocery List

½ lb. Ground Chicken

Salt

Grated Parmesan Cheese

Ground Black Pepper

Olive Oil

1 Onion diced

4 cloves of Garlic chopped

Refrigerated Pasta Dough (for Ravioli or Lasagna cut into squares)

2 Roma Tomatoes diced

½ cup White Wine

1 cup of Chicken Broth

½ cup of Heavy Cream

Pinch of Saffron

2 pats of Butter

Flour

RAVIOLI *Preparation:*

In a bowl, combine ground chicken, ½ onion and 2 cloves of the diced garlic, 2 tbsp of grated Parmesan cheese, 1 tsp salt and 1 tsp pepper, and a tbsp of olive oil. Mix thoroughly.

Lay out pasta. If using lasagna dough, cut into 4-5 inch squares. Fill pasta with about a teaspoon of chicken filling, wet the inside edges, fold over across to form a triangle and pinch to seal the moistened edges. If ravioli won't seal well, wet the pointy edges and fold in toward the center to form a rectangle. It should look like a sealed envelope when you are done with it. Make sure the wet edges have been sealed. Set aside on a plate dusted with flour (so it won't stick to plate) in refrigerator while you prepare sauce.

SAUCE *Preparation:*

In a coverable, deep frying pan, sauté the rest of the garlic and onion and the tomatoes with a dash of salt and pepper in enough olive oil to coat and cover for about 5 minutes until tomatoes begin to get tender. Squash tomatoes with a back of a spoon. Add white wine and chicken broth and stir together. Put heat to medium low. Add ½ tsp of salt and ½ tsp of ground black pepper and stir. Add a pinch of saffron, stir, cover and let simmer for about 20 minutes. During the 20 minutes, coat the pats of butter with flour and set aside.

While sauce is simmering, bring water to a boil in a large pot. Add ravioli and let cook for 7-10 minutes.

BACK TO THE *Sauce:*

At the end of 20 minutes, add the cream and the pats of butter and stir slowly. Put heat to low and add one more tablespoon of flour. Stir to get the larger clumps out and let simmer approximately 10 minutes more, stirring occasionally so the sauce doesn't stick to the bottom of the pan. The sauce should be thick enough to coat the back of a spoon.

Drain the ravioli thoroughly, and then let sit for about 2 minutes to let the ravioli set a little bit so the pasta isn't flimsy. Drizzle sauce over the Ravioli.

TOP WITH SOME PARMESAN CHEESE AND SERVE IT, *Bit@h!*

WORDS OF *Wisdom*

Tomatoes complement cream-based sauces.

Saffron provides a great flavor to cream-based sauces.

White Wine and Cream are complementary.

S&M

(Sides & More)

Salad with your choice of homemade dressing

Steamed or sautéed green vegetable

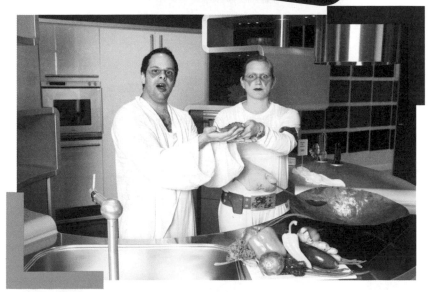

FALLEN ANGELHAIR *Pasta*

(Angel Hair Pasta with Shrimp in a Chorizo Bolgenese)

RATING: DUMB *Ass!*

Grocery List

Olive Oil

¼ Onion diced

3 Garlic cloves chopped

3 Tomatoes diced

¼ cup of Sun Dried Tomatoes

2 Jalapeño Peppers seeded and diced

½ lb. Chorizo

2 sprigs of Cilantro chopped

½ cup of White Wine

3 tbsp of Red Wine Vinegar

Salt

Ground Black Pepper

10-20 thawed frozen, or fresh Shrimp, de-tailed

½ lb. of Angelhair Pasta

S&M

(Sides & More)

Salad with your choice of homemade dressing
Steamed or sautéed green vegetable

Preparation:

In a coverable, semi deep frying pan, sauté garlic and onion in enough olive oil to coat with a dash of salt and pepper for 1-2 minutes until the onions become translucent. Add tomatoes, sun dried tomatoes, and jalapeños and continue to sauté for another minute or so until the tomatoes start to tenderize. Add only a quarter of the chorizo and sauté for an additional minute (this will allow the flavor of the chorizo to be in the sauce, but not all the oil). Add cup of white wine, vinegar and tsp of ½ tsp pepper, and cover. Turn heat to medium low. Let simmer so that tomatoes become tender. Try to "squash" tomatoes with a wooden spoon so that mixture becomes a sauce-like consistency. Simmer for about 45 minutes stirring occasionally.

In another pan, saute the rest of the chorizo in some olive oil for 5-ten minutes then drain the oil when done. Add to sauce towards the end.

Prepare pasta half-way so that it is ready 5 minutes before the sauce is done simmering. Once prepared, put into pan with sauce. If using frozen and thawed, add shrimp for approximately 5 minutes, and stir so that all pasta is coated. If shrimp is fresh, sauté them for five minutes separately in a pan with some olive oil and garlic. Then toss into pasta for an additional five minutes.

SERVE IT, *Bit@h!*

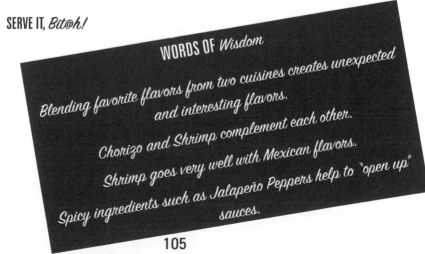

WORDS OF *Wisdom*

Blending favorite flavors from two cuisines creates unexpected and interesting flavors.

Chorizo and Shrimp complement each other.

Shrimp goes very well with Mexican flavors.

Spicy ingredients such as Jalapeño Peppers help to "open up" sauces.

GET BACK IN THE KITCHEN,
Bit@h!
Appetizers

PAN-FRIED GYOZA STUFFED WITH SUN DRIED TOMATOES AND CAPERS WITH A BACON AND TOMATO CREAM DIPPING *Sauce*

Gyoza Wrappers
5 tbsp Sun Dried Tomatoes
3 tbsp Capers
5 Mushrooms
Fresh Parmesan Cheese
2 Garlic cloves finely chopped
2 sprigs Parsley finely chopped
Olive Oil
½ Vidalia Onion chopped finely
1 Roma Tomato
2 strips of Bacon diced finely
½ cup White Wine
½ cup of Chicken Broth
Butter
Salt
Ground Black Pepper
¼ cup Heavy Cream

In a blender, combine ½ cup sun dried tomatoes, 2 tbsp Parmesan cheese, 2 tbsp capers, 4 mushrooms, 1 clove garlic , Vidalia onion and 2 tbsp of Olive Oil. Pulse until a paste is formed. Lay out gyoza wraps. Put a tsp of sun dried tomato mix on wraps. Wet edges of gyoza wraps and pinch and fold together. Set aside on a plate dusted with flour.

In a coverable pan, sauté rest of garlic sun dried tomato, mushrooms, Roma tomato and bacon for 2 to 3 minutes or so. Cover ane let sit for an additional 2 minutes until tomatoes become tender. Squash tomatoes with the back of a spoon and add chicken broth, white wine, and a pinch of salt and pepper. Add butter and bring to a boil for a minute and then simmer. Add tbsp of flour and stir to thicken. Cover and simmer for 10 minutes.

While sauce is simmering, heat enough olive oil to cover the bottom of a separate pan so that the olive oil rises about a quarter of an inch. Pan-fry gyoza for about 2-3 minutes per side so they become golden brown.

While gyoza are being pan-fried, add heavy cream to sauce and mix thoroughly. When gyoza are finished, plate them and drizzle sauce on gyoza.

PROVIDE SAUCE IN A BOWL FOR DIPPING AND SERVE IT, *Bit@h!*

GARLIC BREAD WITH A BALSAMIC *Drizzle*

Loaf of Italian Bread sliced thinly on an angle
3 cloves Garlic finely chopped
¼ cup Olive Oil
2 pats of Butter
Grated Parmesan Cheese
2-3 sprigs fresh Parsley chopped
Salt
Ground Black Pepper
Balsamic Vinegar

In a sauce pan, sauté garlic in the olive oil for about a minute, until garlic starts to brown. Lower heat to low and add the butter. Let butter completely melt, turn off heat and then set aside.

Pre-heat oven to 325 degrees. Dip the slices off bread in the olive oil, butter and garlic mix and place on a greased baking tray. (You can also choose to drizzle the mixture on top). Make sure to get a few bits of garlic on every piece of bread. Sprinkle with Parmesan cheese and fresh parsley. Add a pinch of salt and pepper. Place in oven and bake for about 10-15 minutes until bread starts to brown on the edges.

RIGHT BEFORE YOU SERVE, DRIZZLE BALSAMIC VINEGAR
ON BREAD AND SERVE IT, *Bit@h!*

FRIED WON TONS WITH BRIE AND RASPBERRY *Jam*

Won Ton Wrappers
Brie
Raspberry Jam
Salt
Ground Black Pepper
Garlic Powder
Vegetable Oil

Place won ton wrappers on a plate. Put about a tsp of Brie and raspberry jam in the center. Sprinkle with a pinch of salt, pepper, and garlic powder. Wet the edges of the wrapper and fold over. Pinch to seal.

In a deep pot, fill a quarter to a half way up with vegetable oil and heat oil. To test if oil is hot enough, drop a little piece of the won ton wrapper in. If it starts to bubble around the wrapper, then it is hot enough. Place, don't drop, the won tons in the oil and cook for about

2-3 minutes until they are golden brown. Remove from oil and place on paper towels to get rid of excess oil.

LET THEM COOL FOR A MINUTE OR TWO AND SERVE 'EM, *Bit@h!*

COCONUT PINEAPPLE SHRIMP *Balls*

2 cups of thawed and detailed frozen Shrimp
½ cup of shredded Coconut
2 Jalapeño Peppers seeded and finely diced
4 cloves of Garlic chopped
¼ cup of crushed Pineapple
Salt
Ground Black Pepper
Flour
½ cup Sweet and Sour Sauce
1 tbsp Soy Sauce

In a food processor, combine shrimp, coconut, jalapeño peppers, garlic and pineapple with 1 tsp of salt and ½ tsp of ground black pepper. Add 3 tbsp of flour and blend together until it forms a paste. Wet hands and form small balls (about the size of a Quarter). Lay out flour in a bowl and coat balls on all sides. Set aside.

In a large, deep pot, fill a quarter to a half way up with vegetable oil and heat oil. To test if oil is hot enough, drop a little of the shrimp mixture in. If it starts to bubble around the mixture, then it is hot enough. Place, don't drop, the balls in the oil and cook for about 3 minutes until golden brown. Remove from oil and place on paper towels to get rid of excess oil.

SERVE 'EM WITH A MIX OF SOY AND SWEET AND SOUR SAUCE, *Bit@h!*

ASIAN CHICKEN *Skewers*

4-5 Chicken Breasts
2 tbsp Hoison Sauce
2 tbsp Balsamic Vinegar
3 tbps Soy Sauce
1 tsp Curry Power
1 tsp Chili Powder
1 tsp Garlic Powder
½ tsp Ground Black Pepper
Wooden Skewers

MARINADE

Combine Hoison Sauce, Balsamic Vinegar, Soy Sauce, Curry Powder, Chili Powder, Garlic Powder, and Pepper with ¼ cup water and mix thoroughly.

Cut chicken breasts into thin strips and place in marinade for at least 2 hours, preferably overnight.

PREPARATION

Place chicken strips in a greased baking pan and put into oven for about 30 minutes. During this time, place rest of marinade in a sauce pan and bring to a boil. Let boil for 10- 20 seconds and turn heat to low, cover, and simmer for 15-20 minutes. (This will be the sauce you serve it with.)

When chicken strips are done, let cool to room temperature and skewer.

SERVE 'EM WITH THE SAUCE ON THE SIDE FOR DIPPING, *Bit@h!*

PUMPKIN AND TURKEY STUFFED *Cabbage*

Large Cabbage Leaves
1 lb. Ground Turkey
2 cups Pumpkin Purée
1 cup cooked Rice
1 Egg
Curry Powder
Chilli Powder
½ Onion chopped
2 cloves Garlic chopped
Juice of 1 Lemon
Chicken Broth
Sherry Wine
Butter
Juice of Lemon

CABBAGE *Preparation*

Take the outer leaves off and set aside. You will use them to line your pan in the baking step. Then gently remove 6-10 of the larger leaves or as many as you want to make.

FILLING

In a bowl combine turkey, ½ cup of pumpkin purée, pre-cooked rice, egg, 1 tbsp curry powder, 1 tsp of chili powder, tsp of salt and ½ tsp of pepper. Mix thoroughly and set aside.

111

SAUCE

In a deep pan, sauté garlic and onion in enough olive oil to coat for one minute. Turn heat to medium and add 1 tbsp of curry powder, tsp of chili powder, three tsp of lemon juice and tsp each of salt and pepper. Continue to sauté for another minute. Add 2 cups of chicken broth, 1 cup Sherry wine, 2 pats of butter and stir in rest of lemon juice. Let simmer for 2 minutes or so. Add 1 cup of pumpkin purée, stir to incorporate into sauce and simmer for another two minutes. Take off heat and set aside.

CONSTRUCTING THE STUFFED *Cabbage*

Gently blanche the usable cabbage leaves until pliable. Next, carefully cut out the center vein from the leaves so they will be easier to roll up. Take the reserved big outer leaves and lay them on the bottom of a casserole pan, let part of the leaves hang out the sides of the pan. This insulation will prevent the cabbage rolls from burning on the bottom when baked. Use all the good-looking leaves to make the cabbage rolls. Put about ½ cup of the meat filling in the center of the cabbage and starting at what was the stem-end, fold the sides in, and roll up the cabbage to enclose the filling. Place the cabbage rolls side by side in rows, seam-side down, in a casserole pan.

BAKING

Pre-heat oven to 350 degrees. Pour sauce on top of cabbage rolls and bake for an hour.

SERVE 'EM, *Bit@h!*

● ● ● ● ● ●

TORTILLA ROLLS STUFFED WITH CREAM CHEESE AND *Salsa*

Flour Tortillas
Tub of Vegetable Cream Cheese
1 tsp of Chili Powder
¼ cup favorite Salsa

Place cream cheese in a microwave safe bowl and put in to microwave for 15 seconds to soften it. Add chili powder and salsa and mix thoroughly. Thinly spread mixture on approximately ¾ of the tortilla. Starting from the side where there is cheese spread, roll tortilla tightly. Wrap in plastic wrap and refrigerate for 2 hours. When ready to serve, unwrap plastic wrap and slice with a sharp knife into 1 inch "wheels."

SERVE 'EM, *Bit@h!*

HOW 'BOUT I "GATHER" YOUR ASS, *Bit@h?!?*

113

GET BACK IN THE KITCHEN,
Bit@h!

Sides

DEEP-FRIED SWEET POTATO AND JALAPEÑO *Balls*

2 Sweet Potatoes
2 Jalapeño Peppers
1 tbsp Chili Powder
2 cloves of Garlic
½ Onion chopped
2 strips of Bacon diced
½ cup of shredded Cheddar Cheese
2 tbsp Sour Cream
1 tbsp Flour
1 tsp Salt
1 tsp Ground Black Pepper
2 pats of Butter
Vegetable Oil

Cut sweet potatoes into one-inch slices and boil. Dice jalapeños, garlic and onion finely and set aside.

When sweet potatoes are tender to the fork, place in a bowl while still hot. Add jalapeños, bacon, chili powder, garlic, onion, shredded cheddar cheese, butter, sour cream, salt, pepper, and flour. Mash with masher or back of fork until mixture is smoothed.

Let cool until firm in refrigerator for at least an hour.

Form into "meatball-sized" balls and place on a plate. Heat vegetable oil in deep fryer or deep pot halfway up, on a medium high heat. Make sure oil is very hot before you deep fry (can test with a small amount of potato mixture—if you drop it in, and intense bubbles form around it, it is hot enough.) Carefully place potato balls in the oil and let fry for 3-4 minutes. Remove and place on paper towels, and repeat until all balls are prepared.

BEST TO SERVE 'EM PROMPTLY, *Bit@h!*

ASPARAGUS, SHIITAKE *Custard*

4 Eggs
½ cup Milk
½ cup of Heavy Cream
5 Stalks of Asparagus
3 cloves of Garlic
½ cup of Shiitake Mushrooms
½ Vidalia Onion
Salt
Ground Black Pepper
Cumin Powder

Beat the eggs.

In a blender puree asparagus, garlic shiitake mushrooms, and Vidalia onion with tsp each of salt and pepper, cumin and ¼ cup heavy cream. Heat another ¼ cup cream and milk on medium heat to a slow boil, while stirring.

Take off heat and immediately combine with eggs and stir until smooth. Add the asparagus mixture and mix thoroughly. Dish into small oven safe dish and bake at 325 degrees for approximately 45 minutes or until a knife comes clean out of the center.

DISH IT OUT AND SERVE IT WITH YOUR ENTRÉE, *Bit@h!*

MEXICAN MASHED POTATO SPHERES WITH MINT JALAPEÑO *Sour Cream*

3 Large Russet Potatoes
½ Onion chopped
4 cloves Garlic minced
½ cup of Cheddar Cheese
1-2 Jalapeño Peppers diced
¼ cup whole Corn
Cumin Powder
Paprika
Oregano
Chili Powder
Salt
1 Egg
Flour
Bread Crumbs
Corn Oil
¼ cup of Mexican Beer
¼ cup Red Wine Vinegar

Boil potatoes (can peel if desired, but not necessary) until tender to
the fork. In a bowl combine potatoes, onion, garlic, cheddar, jalapeño,
corn, ½ tbsp each of cumin, paprika, oregano, chilli powder, salt. Add
beer, and 1 tsp flour and mash thoroughly until all mixed. Let cool.
Form balls and set aside. Heat oil in a deep pot (about half way up).
To test if oil is hot enough, take a small amount of potato and place
in the pot. If intense bubbles form around the potato, oil is ready. Lay
out some flour and bread crumbs in two separate plates. Beat egg in a

bowl and dredge balls in flour, then egg then bread crumbs. Place balls carefully into pot for 2-3 minutes each until they become golden brown, and set on to paper towels.

Mint Jalapeño Sour Cream
3 sprigs fresh Mint
2 cloves Garlic
¼ Jalapeño Pepper
3 tbsp of Sour Cream

In a food processor combine all ingredients and thoroughly mix.

PUT A DOLLOP OF SOUR CREAM ON EACH POTATO SPHERE
AND SERVE IT WITH YOUR ENTRÉE, *Bit@h!*

FANCY A SPOT OF TEA, *Bit@h?!?*

117

MEXICAN MASHED *Potatoes*

2 Baking Potatoes
1 Jalapeño Pepper
1 Tomato
½ Onion diced
2 cloves Garlic diced
Cumin Powder
Chili Powder
Salt
Ground Black Pepper
Paprika
Frozen Corn
Lime
Mexican Beer
Red Wine Vinegar
Sour Cream

In a coverable pot, sauté garlic and onion in olive oil with a pinch of salt, pepper, chili powder, and paprika for 1 minute. Add half a bottle/can of beer, ½ cup of vinegar, ½ tbsp each of cumin powder, paprika, chili powder salt and ½ tsp of pepper. Add juice of one lime and bring to a boil. Cut potatoes in quarters and place in liquid. Then bring liquid to a simmer and cover. Cook until potatoes are tender to the fork (approximately 15-20 mins). Place potatoes in a bowl with ½ cup of frozen corn. Strain the liquid into a bowl to separate liquid and cooked vegetables. Add ¼ cup of the hot liquid, 2 dollops of sour cream, the strained garlic, tomatoes, jalapenos, and onions, and mash together.

In a pot, put the leftover liquid from straining and add a pat of butter. Bring to a simmer and add 1 tbsp of flour while stirring. Cover and simmer until thick (about 5-10 minutes).

DRIZZLE ON POTATOES AND SERVE IT WITH YOUR ENTRÉE, *Bit@h!*

SCALLOPED POTATOES WITH HORSERADISH MUSTARD AND *Sour Cream*

2 large Baking Potatoes
1 Onion sliced
2 tbsp Butter
2 ½ tbsp Flour
1 tsp Salt
1/4 tsp Ground Black Pepper
2 cloves Garlic minced
2 cups Milk
½ cup Sour Cream
½ cup of Horseradish Mustard

Peel and finely slice potatoes and onions. Then, in a sauce pan, melt butter at medium heat and add flour, salt, pepper, and minced garlic, stir and cook for about a minute (will be a clump of flour and butter) and add milk and stir constantly until mixture becomes thick and just starts to boil. Take off heat and mix in sour cream and horseradish mustard.

Layer half the potatoes and onions in a casserole dish, cover with sauce. Repeat with second half of potatoes, onions and sauce.

Cover and bake at 350 degrees for 1 hour. Then remove cover, and bake for another ½ hour.

SERVE IT WITH YOUR ENTRÉE, *Bit@h!*

GET BACK IN THE KITCHEN,
Bit@h!
Sauces, Dips, & Salad Dressings

CILANTRO, MINT, AND GARLIC *Remoulade*

½ cup of Cilantro

¼ cup of Mint

4 cloves of chopped Garlic

1 cup of Mayonnaise

1 tbsp Olive Oil

1 tsp Salt

½ tsp of Ground Black Pepper

In a food processor, combine all ingredients until smooth.

SERVE IT WITH CHORIZO SHRIMP CAKES, GARLIC BREAD

OR TORTILLA CHIPS, *Bit@h!*

HORSERADISH MUSTARD, ONION *Dip*

1 cup of Sour Cream

¼ cup of Horseradish Mustard

Packet of Onion Soup Mix

1 tbsp of Parsley Flakes

COMBINE ALL INGREDIENTS IN A BOWL AND MIX 'EM THOROUGHLY, *Bit@h!*

LEMON DILL SALAD *Dressing*

1 cup Mayonnaise
½ tsp Salt
Juice of 1 Lemon
2 sprigs of fresh Dill chopped or ½ tsp of dried Dill
½ tsp Ground Black Pepper
½ tsp of Onion Powder
½ tsp of Garlic Powder

Combine in a bowl and mix together thoroughly. If dressing is too thick, add a little water. Let refrigerate for an hour before serving.

DRIZZLE ON YOUR SALAD, *Bit@h!*

MEXICAN CHILI SALAD *Dressing*

1 cup Mayonnaise
1 tsp Chili powder
½ tsp Salt
½ tsp Ground Black Pepper
Juice of 1 Lime
½ tbsp grated Parmesan Cheese

Combine in a bowl and mix together thoroughly. If dressing is too thick, add a little water. Let refrigerate for an hour before serving.

DRIZZLE ON YOUR SALAD, *Bit@h!*

MEXICAN CHILI SALAD *Dressing II*

¼ cup of Olive Oil
1 tsp Chili powder
½ tsp Salt
½ tsp Ground Black Pepper
Juice of 1 Lime
½ tbsp grated Parmesan Cheese

COMBINE ALL INGREDIENTS IN A BOWL AND MIX THOROUGHLY.
DRIZZLE ON YOUR SALAD, *Bit@h!*

DIJON VINAIGRETTE SALAD *Dressing*

½ cup of Olive Oil
¼ cup of Balsamic Vinegar
3 tbsp of Dijon Mustard
½ tsp of Garlic Powder
½ tsp of Ground Black Pepper
½ tsp of Parsley Flakes
Salt to taste

COMBINE ALL INGREDIENTS IN A BOWL AND MIX THOROUGHLY.
DRIZZLE ON YOUR SALAD, *Bit@h!*

CAESAR DRESSING, *Bit@h Style*

½ cup Mayonnaise
½ tsp Salt
Juice of ½ Lemon
2 tbsp of Red Wine Vinegar
1 tbsp of Garlic Powder
½ tsp Ground Black Pepper
½ tsp of Onion Powder
1 tbsp of grated Parmesan Cheese

COMBINE ALL INGREDIENTS IN A BOWL AND MIX THOROUGHLY, *Bit@h!*

GET BACK IN THE KITCHEN,
Bit@h!
Soups, Chilies, & Stews

GAZPACHO

2 Cucumbers
4 Tomatoes
1 Onion
2 Jalapeño Peppers seeded
1 Red Bell Pepper seeded
3 Garlic cloves
Salt
Ground Black Pepper
Paprika
Cumin
Red Wine Vinegar
Olive Oil

Dice a quarter of the onion, one tomato and 1 garlic clove and set aside. Cut the rest of the vegetables in chunks and put in a blender. Blend until semi smooth. In a pot, sauté the quarter of onion, tomato and garlic clove that you diced, in olive oil for one minute until onions are translucent. Pour blended mixture into pot and bring to a boil for less than a minute. Then simmer. As it's simmering put ½ tsp pepper, salt to taste, ½ tbsp of Paprika and Cumin and stir. Stir in ½ cup of red wine vinegar and let simmer for 20 minutes while stirring. Put into a bowl, cover and chill in fridge until cold.

SERVE COLD WITH A DOLLOP OF SOUR CREAM, *Bit@h!*

PUMPKIN CHILI WITH PORK AND *Bacon*

Vegetable Oil
1 Onion Diced
2 cloves of Garlic diced
Red Wine Vinegar
2 Jalapeño Peppers diced
2 Tomatoes diced
Red Beans
1 lb Ground Pork
2 strips of Bacon diced
1 can Pumpkin Purée
Paprika
Salt
Ground Black Pepper
Chili Powder
Cumin
1 Bay Leaf

In a large pot, sauté onion and garlic in enough vegetable oil to coat with dash of salt and pepper for about 1-2 minutes until onions become translucent. Add 2 tbsp red wine vinegar, jalapeño peppers, tomatoes, ½ tsp each of chili powder and paprika and continue to sauté for another two minutes or so. Add ground pork and bacon and cook until browned. Add pumpkin puree, ½ cup of red wine vinegar, ½ tbsp each of Paprika, Chili powder, cumin, salt, ½ tsp pepper, and 1 bay leaf. Simmer for 2-4 hours.

SERVE WITH A DOLLOP OF SOUR CREAM, *Bit@h!*

POLISH SAUERKRAUT AND KIELBASA *Soup*

You may have just looked at the title of this recipe and thought "What the hell is this bitch thinking?" Well listen up, dumb ass. I thought the same exact thing when I went to Poland with a friend and he told me what I had just ordered. But I have to tell you something you closed-minded piece of trash. This has become one of my favorite soups to make. It's so damn easy, and tastes so damn good.

Vegetable Oil
1 Onion diced
3 cloves Garlic diced
2 Carrots cut into bite-sized chunks
1-2 cups of Sauerkraut
Polish Kielbasa (smoked)
2 cups Chicken Broth
2 cups Water
2 pats of Butter
Salt
Ground Black Pepper
3 sprigs of fresh Dill

In a large pot, sauté onion and garlic in enough vegetable oil to coat for about a minute until the onion becomes translucent. Add carrots and kielbasa and sauté for another minute or two. Add chicken broth, water, butter and salt and pepper to taste (remember that the kielbasa is salted and you don't want to over-salt). Add sauerkraut and dill. Stir and simmer for about 25-30 minutes.

SERVE IT, *Bit@h!*

CHICKEN, BARLEY AND MUSHROOM *Soup*

Olive Oil
½ Onion diced
2 cloves Garlic chopped
Salt
Ground Black Pepper
1 cup Mushrooms sliced or chopped
2 Chicken Breasts cubed
2 Carrots diced
1 cup Barley
4 cups Chicken Broth
3 springs of fresh Dill or ½ tbsp dried Dill
3 cups Water
½ cup of Red Wine Vinegar
1 pat Butter
2-3 tbsp Flour
½ cup of frozen Peas

In a large pot, sauté onion and garlic with a dash of salt and pepper in enough olive oil to coat for about a minute. Add mushrooms and chicken and a swig of red wine vinegar and sauté for another minute until chicken is browned. Add carrots and barley and sauté for another minute. Add chicken stock, dill, water, 1 tsp salt, 1 tsp pepper, and ½ cup of red wine vinegar. Bring to a boil. Cover and turn heat to medium low and simmer for about 30-40 minutes until barley is tender. Add butter and flour and stir to get the major lumps out. Cover and simmer another 5 minutes or so until soup is thickened. About 2 minutes before serving, add frozen peas.

SERVE IT, *Bit@h!*

STUFFED CABBAGE *Soup*

1 cup Rice
½ lb. Ground Meat (Chicken, Beef, Turkey or Pork)
Egg
½ Onion chopped
3 Garlic cloves chopped
Vegetable Oil
Can of diced Tomatoes
2 Carrots diced
4 cups Chicken Broth
Red Wine Vinegar
Tomato Juice
Lemon
Dill
Salt
Ground Black Pepper
3-4 large Cabbage Leaves chopped
1 pat of Butter

Prepare rice by combining the 1 cup of rice with 2 cups of water in a coverable pot. Cover and bring to a boil, then simmer for 10-20 minutes until water has been absorbed. Set aside and let cool.

In a bowl combine the ground meat with 1 cup (approximately 1/3) of the cooled rice, 1 tsp salt and ½ tsp pepper and 1 egg. Mix thoroughly and form into small meat balls. Set aside

In a large stock pot, sauté onion and garlic in enough vegetable oil to coat the bottom of the pan with a dash of salt and pepper. Sauté for about 1 minute. Carefully, without crowding the pot, brown the meatballs for approximately 1-2 minutes on all sides. Brown them in batches, so that when one batch is done, take them out and put the next batch in. Do this until all the meatballs have been browned and they are firm. Deglaze the pot with a little of the chicken broth. Then put all the meatballs back into the pot. Add can of diced tomatoes, carrots, rest of chicken broth, juice of 1 lemon, ¼ cup of red wine vinegar, and 1 cup of tomato juice. Add 5 sprigs of fresh dill or 1 tbsp of dried dill, 1 tsp of ground black pepper and salt to taste (chicken broth and tomato juice have salt already, so use salt sparingly). Bring to a boil for a minute, add cabbage leaves and then simmer for 35 mins. About 2 minutes before you serve put the rest of rice in and pat of butter and stir.

SERVE IT, *Bit@h!*

GET BACK IN THE KITCHEN,
Bit@h!

Side Salads

HOMEMADE *Coleslaw*

½ Green Cabbage
2 Carrots peeled
½ Vidalia Onion
¼ cup Mayonnaise
¼ cup Red Wine Vinegar
1 tbsp Garlic Powder
½ tbsp Salt
½ tsp Ground Black Pepper

In a food processor combine cabbage, carrots, and onion and pulse until evenly chopped. Add mayonnaise, red wine vinegar, garlic powder, salt and pepper and mix it thoroughly.

Put in a bowl and let refrigerate for about an hour until chilled.

SERVE IT, *Bit@h!*

GREEK PASTA *Salad*

2 cups of Orzo pre cooked
½ cup of Black and Green Olives sliced
1 cup of quartered Artichoke Hearts
1 cup of Sun Dried Tomatoes chopped
½ cup of crumbled Feta Cheese
1 cup of Cucumber diced

¼ cup of Olive Oil
¼ cup Red Wine Vinegar
½ tbsp of Salt
½ tbsp of Ground Black Pepper
1 tbsp of Garlic Powder

Combine all ingredients in a bowl and mix thoroughly. Let refrigerate for about an hour. Salt to taste.

SERVE IT, *Bit@h!*

MEDITERRANEAN POTATO *Salad*

Olive Oil
4 Red Potatoes diced
½ Onion diced
½ cup frozen cut Green Beans
¼ cup of Capers
2 cups Artichoke Hearts, quartered
1 Tomato diced
¼ cup light Mayonnaise
Red Wine Vinegar
Paprika
Salt
Ground Black Pepper
Parsley Flakes
Dill (fresh or dried)

POTATO *Preparation:*

In a frying pan, sauté potatoes and ¼ of the diced onion in olive oil using ½ tsp each of salt, pepper, paprika and approximately 2 tbsp of vinegar. Sauté until the potatoes are tender to the fork (approximately

10-15 mins). Then allow to cool in a refrigerator until at least room temperature.

DRESSING *Preparation:*

In a small bowl combine the mayonnaise, 3 tbsp red wine vinegar, ½ tsp each of paprika, pepper, parsley flakes, and dill, and pinch or two of salt and mix thoroughly. Add more vinegar if you need/like a tangier sauce.

SALAD *Preparation:*

Defrost frozen green beans by running them under hot water. Allow to dry. In a bowl combine potatoes, green beans, capers, artichokes, tomato, and mix with dressing thoroughly.

Chill in refrigerator for at least an hour.

SERVE IT, *Bit@h!*

GET DOWN TONIGHT, *Bit@h!*

131

CURRY MUSTARD SWEET POTATO *Salad*

2-3 medium Sweet Potatoes
¼ Onion chopped
2 Eggs
¼ cup frozen Peas thawed
¼ cup Light Mayonnaise
Juice of half a Lemon
¼ cup Dijon Mustard
1 tbsp of Curry Powder
½ tsp Chili powder
½ tsp Ground Black Pepper
1 tsp Garlic Powder
½ tsp Salt

In a pot place 2-3 quartered sweet potatoes and 2 eggs. Cover with water and bring to a boil. It is important when boiling eggs to place the eggs in the pot before you turn the heat on as they will rupture if you put them into boiling water. Boil eggs for 15 minutes or so, and take out of water. Keep potatoes boiling for approximately 20 minutes or until you can drive a fork in them easily. When they are done, put potatoes and eggs aside until they are cool.

In a large bowl combine ¼ chopped onion, peas, juice of ½ lemon, ¼ cup of mayonnaise, ¼ cup of Dijon mustard, curry powder, chili powder, salt, garlic powder, ground black pepper, cooled sweet potatoes, cooled eggs. Using a large fork, chop potatoes and eggs into bigger chunks. Then mix thoroughly making sure chunks of potato are in tact. Salt to taste.

JUST EAT THE DAMN THING, *Bit@h!*

GET BACK IN THE KITCHEN, *Bit@h!*

Desserts

I will be the first to admit: This bitch doesn't bake. I never was able to get it right, as baking requires exact precision, and I use the "little of this, little of that" method to cook. Just coming up with the measurements for this book was a helluva challenge for me. So when it comes to baking and desserts, I leave it up to the pastry chefs.

Whenever I throw a dinner party, I assign desserts to some other bitch. However, over the years, I have found a few tricks that require no-baking. I also found that homemade ice cream is very forgiving and as such, have been able to master that too. So for those of you bitches who can't bake either... here are a few desert recipes that are simple and don't require the oven to be turned on!

YOGURT POUND CAKE *Pudding*

1 cup of Blueberries
2 Bananas sliced
1 can of Pineapple chunks and half the juice of the can
1 cup of Strawberry Yogurt
1 tsp of Cinnamon
1 Pound Cake cut into 2 inch cubes

Combine the fruit, yogurt, and Cinnamon in a bowl and mix thoroughly. Refrigerate for about an hour or so. Approximately 10 mins before you serve put the pound cake squares in and mix so that yogurt mixture coats the pound cake.

SERVE IT, *Bit@h!*

RASPBERRY ALMOND FROZEN *Custard*

You really need an ice cream-maker for this, but it may be possible to freeze the custard and then allow it to melt a little before you serve it. While it melts, you can stir it thoroughly to make it soft.

3 Egg Yolks
2 Eggs
½ cup of Sugar
1 ½ cups Milk
1 ½ cups of Heavy Cream
1 tsp Vanilla Extract
1 tsp Almond Extract
3 heaping tbsp of Raspberry Jam
Chocolate Chip Cookies

Combine the milk and the cream in a pot with the vanilla and almond extract. Heat on medium heat until it comes to a slow boil.

Meanwhile, in a bowl combine the eggs and egg yolks with the sugar. With an electric hand mixer, blend the eggs and sugar on medium speed until the mix becomes pale yellow (about 2-3 minutes.)

When the milk and cream mixture comes to a slow boil, pour approximately 1 cup of it into the egg and use the mixer to blend thoroughly. Then pour the rest of the egg into the pot. Stir and mix thoroughly. Add the raspberry jam and stir thoroughly until jam has melted and mixed in thoroughly.

Pour the mixture into a bowl and place plastic wrap over the bowl so that it is touching the mix so there is no air between mix and plastic wrap. Place in fridge and let it cool completely. I like to leave it in the refrigerator overnight.

When it is cooled, place the custard into your ice cream maker and turn on. It should be ready in 20-30 minutes.

If you don't have an ice cream maker, place bowl of custard in the freezer and let freeze completely. Take it out about an hour or two before you serve it and let melt. As it melts, stir in the melted portion with the frozen portion until it becomes soft.

SERVE IT, *Bit@h!*

FRUIT SALAD WITH YOGURT *Dressing*

1 can of Pineapple chunks
1 cup of Blueberries
2 Bananas sliced
Half of Cantaloupe in one-inch chunks
Half of Honeydew Melon in one-inch chunks
2 cups of Grapes sliced
2 tbsp Lemon Juice
1 cup Strawberry Yogurt
1 tsp of Cinnamon

PLACE ALL INGREDIENTS IN A BOWL AND MIX IT THOROUGHLY, *Bit@h!*

GET BACK IN THE KITCHEN, *Bit@h!*

Prep Recipes

This section is dedicated to stocks, broths, and sauces that you can make ahead of time. Just make them when you have time, and then freeze 'em. When they are needed to make sauces, gravies, or soups for a quick meal, simply defrost. Think you can handle that bitch?!? Let's find out.

DIFFERENCE BETWEEN STOCK AND *Broth*

One of the most common questions I get from you dumb-ass bitches is: "What is the difference between stock and broth?" Well, the answer, like you, is quite simple. A stock is made from the meat and the bones of meat, while a broth uses just the meat. Not to get too technical, because I know your simple mind won't be able to comprehend, but as a result of the collagen in the bones, a stock will become jellied when it chills, and broths won't.

CHICKEN *Stock*

Vegetable Oil
½ Onion diced
2 cloves Garlic chopped

2 Carrots diced
1 stalk of Celery diced
Salt
Ground Black Pepper
Two Chicken legs or thighs
8 cups Water

In a large pot, sauté onion and garlic in enough vegetable oil to coat with dash salt and pepper for about a minute. Add carrots and celery and sauté for another minute. Brown chicken legs or thighs. Add water, 1 tsp salt, 1 tsp pepper and bring to a boil. Cover, set heat to medium low and simmer for 1-2 hours. Let cool in refrigerator (overnight is best, but for at least three hours). Take chicken out. Strain into a storage container to remove vegetables and excess fat. You can refrigerate or freeze vegetables and chicken for use in a soup or stew or even stir-fry later.

BEEF *Broth*

Vegetable Oil
½ Onion diced
2 cloves Garlic chopped
2 Carrots diced
1 stalk of Celery diced
Salt
Ground Black Pepper
½ lb. of Pot-roast or other tough/cheap cut of meat
8 cups Water

In a large pot, sauté onion and garlic in enough vegetable oil to coat with dash salt and pepper for about a minute. Add carrots and celery and sauté for another minute. Brown meat. Add water, 1-2 tsps salt (your preference), 1 tsp pepper and bring to a boil. Cover, set heat to medium low and simmer for about 2 hours. Let cool in refrigerator (overnight is best, but for at least three hours). Take beef out. Strain into a storage container to remove vegetables and excess fat. You can refrigerate or freeze vegetables and beef for use in another dish later.

You can use the same recipes for meat or vegetable stocks or broths. The only difference is the meat used. Also, remember if you are making a stock, use the bones of the meat, if it's a broth, just the meat.

Another way to cut time in the kitchen is to always have some tomato sauce on hand. This is great if you want to whip up a quick pasta dish, or even a pizza. The following is an easy recipe for a tomato sauce that you can make and freeze.

EASY TOMATO *Sauce*

½ Onion diced
4 cloves Garlic chopped
5 Roma Tomatoes diced
10-15 Grape Tomatoes halved
1 can Tomato Paste
½ cup Wine (Red, White or Marsala: Red makes a sweeter, more traditional sauce, but White or Marsala gives a great unexpected flavor)
Juice of 1 Lemon
½ tsp of Sugar
Salt
Ground Black Pepper
Crushed Red Pepper flakes
3 tbsp Parmesan Cheese
¼ cup of fresh Parsley or Parsley flakes

Optional Vegetables to put into Sauce
Diced Eggplant
Diced Mushrooms
Diced Celery
Diced Carrots
Diced Zucchini

In a pot, sauté onion and garlic in enough olive oil to coat with dash salt and pepper for about a minute. Add roma tomatoes and grape tomatoes and sauté on medium to medium-high heat for another two minutes until tomatoes start to "melt" or break down. I like to mash them a bit at this point so the fibers start to become sauce-like. Add a few swigs of wine to deglaze pot and stir. Add tomato paste and begin to stir until it becomes "sauce-like." Add ½ cup of wine, lemon juice (can substitute 3 tbsp of vinegar here) and sugar and stir until everything becomes consistent. Add salt and pepper to taste and a few sprinkles of crushed red pepper, and Parmesan cheese. Cover, set heat to medium low and simmer for about 45 minutes to an hour, stirring occasionally. About 10 minutes before finishing, add the parsley or parsley flakes, and stir.

● ● ● ● ●

LEARNING TO LOVE YOUR LEFTOVERS...*Again!*

So you went ahead and made a whole heap of Chicken Marsala, and as piggish as you and your family are, you couldn't finish the damn thing. You say to yourself: "What the heck am I gonna do with all these damn leftovers? No one likes leftover night. Hmmm, maybe I'll just cut my losses and throw it out?" You stupid bitch. Don't you dare ever let me hear you say that again. The fact is that you can take your leftovers and create a whole new meal that you and whatever freeloaders you feed are going to love to eat again! There are some really simple tips that you can follow.

First off, it's so easy to disguise flavors by adding new spices and sauces into the mix. For example, that Chicken Marsala can easily be re-used in an Asian stir-fry. The soy sauce and vinegar you would use can easily mask the Marsala flavor, and actually enhance it. Basically, what you want to aim to do, is strengthen the flavors in your new meal, while complementing the taste of the old one. "Strong" flavors are those that are bitter, sour, or salty. Examples are vinegar, soy sauce, and tomato sauce. Chicken Marsala leftovers can be cut up and mixed with tomato sauce and placed on pasta for instance.

140

Leftovers can also be great as a soup or stew. Nothing says "you're adequate" to your loved ones more than a piping hot bowl of stew made from leftovers. These make great meals. If you have chicken, beef or any other leftover meats, simply sauté some vegetables in a pot, add some wine and broth and cut the meat up and let it stew for a couple of hours. It really is that easy, bitch!

Leftover meat can also be great in casseroles. Buffalo chicken and any other spicy meats can be combined with cooked rice or pasta, fresh or frozen vegetables, complementary spices, some cream-based soup, and then baked for about 45 minutes.

Have some leftover meatloaf? A great way to re-use meatloaf is to make an awesome Shepherd's Pie out of it. All you have to do is break down the meatloaf, sauté it in some olive oil with a couple dashes of Worcestershire sauce, place it in a baking dish and top it with mashed potatoes and bake it for about 25 minutes.

SAUCES, GRAVIES, AND BROTHS, *Oh My!*

Let's say you were a stupid bitch and made too much gravy, broth or tomato sauce. What are you gonna do with it? I don't know exactly what answer you have in your head right now, but I bet whatever it is, it's spot-on WRONG. The only acceptable answer would be this: You gather up the leftover sauces in some plastic containers and you freeze the damn things. This way, the next time you come home from a long day of walking the street or pole dancing, you can use the gravy or tomato sauce on pasta, in a stew, or even a casserole. Simply pop the frozen delight into a pan, cover, and heat it on medium low, stirring occasionally until it is defrosted. Then toss it on pasta or a piece of thick, juicy meat. Throw some rice, meat, and the defrosted sauce in a casserole dish and bake the damn thing for a colossal casserole, or sauté some vegetables and beef, pour the gravy on top, and simmer for a scintillating stew.

Here are some ideas to get you started, bitch. We all know you need as much help as you can garner.

MOO-SHOO *Chicken*

A great way to use leftover chicken is to make it into an awesome dish called "Moo-shoo Chicken." This dish is pretty popular in East- and West-Coast Asian establishments, but I have found that many of you in the Mid West and Plains States have yet to experience it. It's so damn easy to make and will work with most of your leftover chicken dishes. Here's what you need:

Sesame Oil

cup of Onions sliced

3 Garlic cloves chopped

¼ to ½ Green Cabbage shredded

cup of Mushrooms chopped

½ cup of any other Chinese vegetable (Bamboo Shoots, Water Chestnuts, or Baby Corn work great)

2 tbsp of Hoison Sauce

1 tbsp of Soy Sauce

1 tbsp of Vinegar

¼ cup of Water

leftover Chicken diced

Flour Tortillas

Start by sautéing the onions and garlic in some sesame oil. Add the rest of the vegetables, sauces, water, and your leftover chicken. Stir, cover, and simmer for about 15-20 minutes and then serve it in the flour tortillas.

CHICKEN AND RICE *Casserole*

Most leftover chicken dishes go great in a chicken and rice casserole. Throw some cooked rice, leftover chicken, frozen vegetables, and some cream based soup into a bowl. Be sure to flavor it with some hot pepper sauce or lemon juice. Mix it thoroughly and put it into a casserole dish with some bread crumbs on top. Shove it into the oven for about 25 minutes, and voila, bitch!

CHICKEN TORTILLA *Stew*

You always have the "stew" option when you deal with leftovers. Again, the trick is to mask any of the original flavors with one's that are bolder. I have found that Mexican flavorings can disguise just about anything. So, if you have some leftover chicken, a great option is to make a Mexican Chicken Tortilla Stew.

Start out by sautéing some onions and garlic in a deep pot. Add chunks of your leftover chicken, some jalapeño peppers, chili powder, cumin, a can of diced tomatoes, some frozen corn, a little orange or pineapple juice, the juice of a lime, and a touch of water. Then, let it simmer for about 40 minutes or so. At the end, grind up some corn tortillas (or even use tortilla chips), throw 'em in and let cook for about 3-5 minutes more. At the end, toss on a few of those tortilla chips. It's that damn easy.

BEEF AND BARLEY *Stew*

Speaking of stews, if you have some leftover beef or steak, just brown some onions and garlic alongside the leftover chunks of beef in a deep pot. Add some frozen veggies and some diced potatoes. Let brown for about 2 minutes and then add a cup of red wine, a cup of beef broth, salt, pepper, garlic powder, a bay leaf, and whatever other spice you may have lying around (be liberal with the spices-except for the salt).

Add a few swigs of Worcestershire sauce and let simmer. Meanwhile, cook a cup of barley. This takes about 35-40 minutes. When it's ready, add the barley to the stew and let simmer for about ten minutes more.

Start with these recipes and then try to expand your repertoire. Don't be affraid to get creative with your leftovers and make some amazing new things. Even you can learn to be a real bitch in the kitchen with your leftovers, so don't cop out anymore. Got it? Good.

● ● ● ● ● ● ● ●

EN GARDE, *Bit@h!*

SO, YOU'RE STILL TOO DAMN LAZY TO START FROM *Scratch?*

As you may imagine, I am pretty freakin' busy trying to keep you bitches in line. There are some nights that I get home after yelling at you on Facebook, or answering all of your damn culinary questions, that I just want to be in and out of the kitchen in less than a half an hour. But that doesn't mean I have to order in crap, or sacrifice my taste buds by heating up a salty can of soup. Instead, I have found some great ways to make succulent meals by using what G-d gave me... packaged foods.

In the last book, I taught you a few great recipes using Rice-a-Foni, frozen pizzas, and cans of soup. Well, now I am going to teach you more of those and some new casseroles that I have been perfecting as well. Don't be a lazy bitch anymore, try these out!

SIMPLE *Paella*

½ Onion diced
2 cloves Garlic diced
2 Roma Tomatoes diced
Spanish Rice-a-Foni
2 cups frozen Shrimp (thawed and de-tailed)
1 cup Roasted Red Peppers diced
Saffron

In a semi-deep frying pan sauté onion, roasted red pepper, tomatoes and garlic in enough olive oil to coat with dash salt and pepper for about a minute until the onions become translucent. Add rice from box of rice-a-foni and sauté for another minute or so until the rice becomes translucent. Add 2 cups of water, contents of half of the Spanish rice seasoning packet, and a pinch of saffron. Stir and bring to a boil. As soon as water begins to boil, turn heat to medium-low, cover, and let simmer for about 10 minutes. Add Shrimp, and re-cover to allow the rest of the water to be absorbed into the rice. Once rice has absorbed all the water, stir for a few minutes.

SIMPLE *Cajun*

½ Onion diced
2 cloves Garlic diced
2 Roma Tomatoes diced
1 cup Green Bell Peppers diced
Chicken Rice-a-Foni
3-5 Hot Dogs sliced
can of Red Beans
tsp each of Paprika, Chili Powder
pinch of Cayenne Pepper
3 tbsp of Red Wine Vinegar

In a semi-deep frying pan sauté onion, green pepper, tomatoes and garlic in enough olive oil to coat with a dash of salt and pepper for about a minute until the onions become translucent. Add rice from box of rice-a-foni and sauté for another minute or so until the rice becomes translucent. Add 2 cups of water, contents of half of the chicken seasoning packet, hot dogs, red beans, paprika, chili powder, cayenne pepper, and red wine vinegar. Stir and bring to a boil. As soon as water begins to boil, turn heat to medium-low, cover, and let simmer for about 20 minutes until the water has been absorbed into the rice. Once rice has absorbed all the water, stir for a few minutes.

RICE-A-FONI *Casserole*

1 Onion diced
2 Chicken Breasts diced
Rice-a-Foni (Chicken or Pilaf Flavor)
frozen or fresh Cut Green Beans
frozen Peas
frozen Corn
Ground Black Pepper
Hot Pepper Sauce
Garlic Powder
1 can of Cream of Chicken Soup
Juice of half of a Lemon
½ cup of Bread Crumbs

In a semi deep frying pan, sauté onions in enough olive oil to coat with a dash of ground black pepper for about 2 minutes until onions become translucent. Add chicken and sauté for another minute or so. Add 2 tsp of hot pepper sauce and 1 tsp of garlic powder. Add dry rice from mix and sauté until rice becomes translucent (about 1-2 minutes.) Add 2 cups of water and ¼-½ of flavor packet and stir. Bring to a boil, cover and set heat to medium low and simmer until all liquid is absorbed into rice.

Meanwhile, grease a (9x9 inch) baking pan. Preheat oven to 350 degrees. When rice is done pour into baking pan along with soup, green beans, peas, and corn. Add ¼ cup of bread crumbs (leaving rest for top of casserole), 2 tbsp of hot pepper sauce, lemon juice and mix thoroughly. Top with rest of breadcrumbs and bake for 20-30 minutes.

STUFFED CABBAGE *Soup*

In the soups section of this book, there is a recipe for "Stuffed Cabbage Soup" from scratch. Well, now we can cheat a bit. If you don't have time to make the chicken broth, and the meatballs, a really easy way to simulate this is with a can of soup that already has meatballs in it. So, pick up some soups that contain meatballs damn it! Italian Wedding Soup, for instance. There is also one that I find ideal for this dish. I won't name it by name because of trademark laws, and I don't want the stupid bitches to sue me. However, the company that makes it starts with a "P," ends with an "O" and rhymes with "digresso." The soup has chicken, vegetables, meatballs and little balls of pasta in it. Good luck finding it.

To make the soup, sauté some onions, and about one diced chicken breast with a can of diced tomatoes. Add the soup and a few cans of water. Add the juice of one lemon or about ¼ cup of vinegar to the mix and stir. When it starts to boil, throw in about 5 chopped cabbage leaves and some dill, cover and let simmer. You should also add some frozen veggies of your choice to make the soup more substantial. Add more vinegar and salt to taste. I also love to sprinkle some Parmesan cheese on top.

Between this book and the last one, you should now have some great ideas of how to use pre-made, packaged food to come up with quick home-cooked meals. But I can't do all the damn work for you. Take what you have learned and come up with some of your own. I am giving you permission to take short cuts here. Nothing says that you have to always start from scratch to be a good cook. Don't be a freakin' martyr anymore.

AT EASE. YOU ARE
DISMISSED, *Bit@h!*

Throughout the years, cooks have been developing innovative methods for preparing food so they could eat things that taste good and subsequently not starve to death. Some have used fire, some have used ovens, and some have even used blow torches. But make no mistake about it. They were all bitches. And now, you too have become a real bitch in the kitchen. You have learned some new techniques, understood what tools can help you prepare food more efficiently, and under my tutelage, have generally improved yourself. I am proud to have been instrumental in your progression from the piece of crap cook you once were, to the slightly more advanced idiot that you have become. But stay tuned bitch, I am not done with you yet.

Don't be afraid to take what you have learned and apply these lessons to make your own creative dishes. Don't be a wimpy bitch anymore...you can do it. I know. I taught you well, and I am damn confident in my skills. I'm done with you, and for now... YOU ARE *Dismissed!*

PHOTO *Gallery*

PHOTO *Gallery*

PHOTO *Gallery*

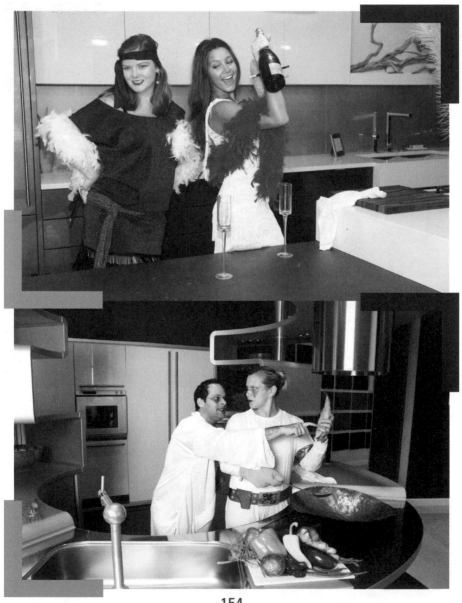

PHOTO *Gallery*

RECIPE *Listing*

WRITE YOUR OWN RECIPE
HERE, *Bit@h!*

WRITE YOUR OWN RECIPE
HERE, *Bit@h!*

WRITE YOUR OWN RECIPE HERE, *Bit@h!*